ASTRAKHAN (WINTER)

to the memory of

Dan, my father

and

Shane, my lost student

Dic Edwards

ASTRAKHAN (WINTER)
the fourth world
MANIFEST DESTINY
Poems

OBERON BOOKS
LONDON

First published in 2005 by Oberon Books Ltd.

521 Caledonian Road, London N7 9RH

Tel: 020 7607 3637 / Fax: 020 7607 3629

e-mail: oberon.books@btinternet.com

www.oberonbooks.com

A catalogue record for this book is available from the British Library.

ISBN: 9781840025965

Cover illustration: Andrzej Klimowski

Contents

ASTRAKHAN
(WINTER)

Characters

WALKER
an historian

LUKE
his son

GRACE
his wife

SMERDYAKOV
a refugee

NATASHIA
a nightclub singer

FRAN
Grace's lover

Ghost of ALYOSHA
a dead partisan

Ghost of LEBEDEV
a dead leader of the partisans

Ghost of GRUSHENKA
a dead student of Lebedev's

Ghost of SONIA
a dead student of Lebedev's

Astrakhan (*Winter*) was first performed by Cambridge Amateur Dramatic Club at The Edinburgh Festival Fringe on 7 August 2005 at C Venue 34 on Chamber Street, with the following actors:

Sarah Bird

Hermione Buckland-Holy

Stephanie Cohen

Ed Coleman

Monique Cornwell

Tim Dickinson

Allegra Galvin

Jay Millar

Luke Roberts

Oliver Robinson

Adam Welch

Director James Dacre

Producer Eve Williams

Designer Lucy Styles

Composer Jonathan Styles

Musical Director Joe Adams

Musical and Sound Director Ned Beauman

Lighting Designer Simon Hicks

Assistant Producer Oliver Tilley

Assistant Designers Lucy Minyo, Benjamin Seidler and
    Olly Wainwright

Stage and Publicity Manager Kay Drage

Scene One

A mountaintop.

WALKER and GRACE. Wind in hair. (A swirling effect – from the mountaintop wind to the dancing to the confusion of reported speeches – should try to be achieved.)

GRACE: Your student.

WALKER: Stepan?

GRACE: The Russian, yes.

WALKER: Stepan Smerdyakov.

GRACE: When will he arrive?

WALKER: Wednesday.

    (Pause.)

GRACE: I love it here. This mountaintop. It's...all the memories.

WALKER: It's so much like Kalmytskaya. Those Caucasus. *(Pause.)* I want to be...cleansed. Reborn. I am going to write my book. It will be the final word. On everything. Including history.

GRACE: I think the war changed you.

WALKER: Why did you leave? Me.

GRACE: Many things.

WALKER: Can it be as it was? With us. That would help. My healing.

GRACE: I want to. And you have changed. Even in the months since you've returned you've changed.

WALKER: I hope it's true. For the better. It's not for me to say. I hope with Stepan's visit you'll be able to tell. Have it confirmed. And then we can...re-commit.

    (Pause.)

GRACE: Did you think of me? In the Caucasus. On the mountaintop.

WALKER: I was breaking down. Having a break down. I left here not just as an historian but TV personality! And then I went to Kalmytskaya. And...things happened. To me.

GRACE: The suffering?

WALKER: It's hard to keep a hold.

(*Pause.*)

GRACE: Will you meet Luke?

WALKER: He's my son. That's something I've decided, yes. I will meet him. Did anyone visit him in prison?

GRACE: I don't know. I was estranged. I was afraid. It was only six months. I knew that soon he would be out. I was so afraid. One day I went there. Stood outside the prison. I couldn't go in. It was a bad time. My certainties were failing me. Dying. I am his mother. Though step-mother. His mother. In chains. Even now I am so uncertain.

(*The Ghost of ALYOSHA enters.*)

(*Gasps.*) Did you feel that? A breeze but more like a feeling.

WALKER: I felt nothing.

ALYOSHA: (*To audience.*) The last time I saw this man Walker was the evening before I died. I was one of the partisans. He was one of our heroic leaders. Our leaders were academics. Intellectuals. Like Walker the historian who led us with an almost accidental determination as though he had fallen into our arms.

WALKER: There were times when *I* felt less than certain.

GRACE: In your war?

WALKER: Not really my war. But then, yes. At that time. An insane time.

ALYOSHA: It was a time of purpose driven by our leader in the field, Lebedev, a Professor of poetry who held open his arms to justice. But for me, my throat was slit. I am Alyosha. One of the partisans.

WALKER: I made a speech and they made me a leader! If you enter a village in a tank then there's certainty. But we would enter armed with not much more than belief...

GRACE: But we need belief!

ALYOSHA: I believed! And I never believed more than during the events of that last day. We were in a burnt out school: myself and professor Lebedev and the women, Grushenka and Sonia.

(*The Ghosts of LEBEDEV, GRUSHENKA and SONIA enter.*)

The women were students of the theatre. On this evening they were dancing, performing a piece for Lebedev. For us!

(The women dance (Russian music).
They come together, kiss etc.)

GRUSHENKA: In my death
I will live the days when
My grandfather's grandfather sold ribbons in Baku

SONIA: and the Caspian held
All the immeasurable bearing of Spring.

GRUSHENKA: In my death
I will live the days when
My grandfather's grandfather sold ribbons in Baku

SONIA: And the birds of the littoral
Gave a chorus to our singing.

ALYOSHA: I saw that Walker had arrived. With his student
Stepan Smerdyakov. These two were so close! Like father
and son. Walker signalled me that he didn't want to be
seen. He watched us as Lebedev shouted joyously:

LEBEDEV: I love that! Grandfather's grandfather! One
hundred years ago at the turn of the old century; in the
days before the depredations of the twentieth – the billion
dead; before high capitalism when life was about the
handling of ribbon. And Grushenka said:

GRUSHENKA: And before the Soviet despotism! And Sonia
said:

SONIA: But were those days so good? Isn't that too romantic?

ALYOSHA: And Lebedev said – forcefully:

LEBEDEV: No! Listen! Don't accuse us of that! There has
always been suffering. Especially in those old days: the
days of the Tzar. No! We fight with a new consciousness.
We fight for beauty!

ALYOSHA: I was nervous; cautious! Would Walker want
to hear this? And I said: Beauty! But war is ugly! And
Lebedev said:

LEBEDEV: Beauty isn't simply the opposite of ugliness! We
find beauty in the reconciliation of opposites; unity! – just
as in poetry; in art! Those ribbons – they become symbols
don't they, of what we don't want to lose. The ribbon
makers! The painters! The poets! Ideas meet in symbols
and remind us of our quest; of our movement towards

goals. And one of those goals is beauty and beauty holds in its embrace suffering and knowledge. There is oil yet forty-seven per cent of our people live in poverty. That is a fact. Knowledge! We have suffered but we know our future! (*Pause.*) And now I would like to dance!

ALYOSHA: And the women embraced him saying:

WOMEN: You are our leader professor and we love you! (*They dance again.*)

ALYOSHA: Then Walker and Smerdyakov entered. I was sure Walker would have been angry standing there watching the dancing and I shouted: We shouldn't be doing this! Look who's here! Aren't we trivialising things? And Grushenka said angrily:

GRUSHENKA: Today we fought, now we are giving a performance. For Professor Lebedev. And for Professor Walker!

ALYOSHA: And Sonia said:

SONIA: This is our revolution Alyosha! A revolution of the artists! If you don't like it you should go back to school!

ALYOSHA: And I said, with an eye on Walker to watch for his reaction: this weakens us! And Lebedev said:

LEBEDEV: Nonsense! It's theatre!

ALYOSHA: And Grushenka said to Walker:

GRUSHENKA: Do you feel threatened by this? And Walker said to Lebedev warmly:

WALKER: What are they? Your lovers? Mistresses? And he said:

LEBEDEV: They are my students! And we are on the threshold of beauty!

WALKER: And I said: well I hope so!

SONIA: And I said to Alyosha: Don't you understand? We must have this! We are suffering! Our country is ruined. We want the truth!

ALYOSHA: Then Lebedev said to me:

LEBEDEV: You are not a poet Alyosha. The truth is something else for you!

GRUSHENKA: And I said (*To ALYOSHA.*) Perhaps you've done all you can for us. Perhaps it's time for you to go!

ALYOSHA: (*To audience.*) You must understand: this is how I remember it. It may not be accurate; everything became a blur though I do remember this: Walker said:

WALKER: No! Alyosha is right!

ALYOSHA: Then there was a short silence – I remember this because at that moment there was a distant explosion and then Smerdyakov said so deliberately: 'I think that this belief in beauty is important!' That's exactly what he said as though contradicting Walker: 'I think this belief in beauty is important!' And then Walker said, perhaps annoyed with Smerdyakov:

WALKER: We are in the process of creating YOUR history! This process is unfinished! Let me remind you of the words of Michelet: 'with the world began a war which will end only with the world; the war of man against nature, of spirit against matter, of liberty against fatality. History is nothing other than the record of this interminable struggle.' And I will say: beauty is not part of this history. We can't afford this self-indulgence. We must first win. Your words Lebedev are very powerful. The women are weak with admiration. But don't let them weaken us.

ALYOSHA: That evening we moved on and came to the village of the women.

LEBEDEV: And I remember thinking before I died: we have come too close to freedom.

GRUSHENKA: Later, we were ambushed.

SONIA: Assassinated.

(*Silence.*
Wind.
The ghosts leave.)

WALKER: (*To GRACE.*) Let's put all the uncertainty behind us. (*Pause.*) Yes?
(*WALKER embraces GRACE who reciprocates.*
Lights down.)

Scene Two

Outside a prison. Morning. WALKER, dapper, waiting.

After a moment, sound of heavy door shutting. LUKE, cat-like, acute but uncertain, comes on. He pauses, surprised to see WALKER.

LUKE: (*Short pause.*) I didn't expect... Didn't think I'd ever see you.

WALKER: Forgive me, Luke. The prodigal father.
(*Silence.*
WALKER moves towards LUKE.
WALKER tentatively holds out his arms.)
It's been a hard time. All our lives.
(*He suddenly, almost exaggeratedly, throws his arms around LUKE.*
He is tearful.)

LUKE: I've just done six months. GBH. It was an honourable action. A woman's honour. I could have killed him. But didn't for another consideration. You. My consideration for you. This father. Though I could not give you a breakdown of the reasoning that led to this consideration. I understand you not visiting. You deserved better. It's a cross I made you carry.
(*WALKER releases LUKE.*)

WALKER: A visit wouldn't have helped. But now it's different. I'm stronger. Things have changed. Shall we go for some coffee?

LUKE: I'm waiting for someone.

WALKER: I'll wait. It'll give us a chance to talk. What was the regime in there?

LUKE: Fascist. Chains. Solitary confinement. (*Pause.*) I was sharing a cell with a Romanian.

WALKER: What had he done?

LUKE: Being here. He was skint. He strangled a sheep.

WALKER: Strangled?

LUKE: Yeh. That is strength beyond.

WALKER: He strangled a sheep! I just can't imagine that!

LUKE: Brutalescu. That's what we called him.

WALKER: And he was caught in the process?

LUKE: No. No. A friend of a friend told him of a tiled floor, a tiled floor in the home of a yet further friend. Whoever heard of a Romanian having a friend let alone a network. A copper was in the bathroom doing no one knows what and he leaves the bathroom to find the Romanian shearing his sheep in the hallway. To prepare it for the grilling to come.

(*Silence.*)

You know. Christmas in there. And New Year. New Year's Eve and all the guys will kiss each other. Got to kiss something. Then I thought – I haven't been kissed all year. I'm looking at Brutalescu and he's got huge like brown eyes, all wet looking at me with those wet eyes. So I kiss him. I kiss him like I've never kissed anything before. A really deep kiss. And that's it.

(*Pause.*)

WALKER: It's nippy. (*Pause.*) When will your person come?

LUKE: I don't know if she will.

(*Pause.*)

WALKER: I'd like you to come home Luke. It will help you. Rehabilitate.

(*Silence.*)

Listen, as far as I'm concerned, the past belongs to the past.

LUKE: The past doesn't die.

WALKER: At best it's like the man said: the past is a fiction we've taken to our hearts. (*Short pause.*) If you're worried that at any time I may, for the purpose of...I don't know... gaining some advantage, resurrect it – just put that out of your mind.

LUKE: What about history? You're an historian.

WALKER: From history we learn only how to behave badly: history is not informed by charity. I've come to see it as an unnecessary evil.

LUKE: That's a big change. When I was on remand you said the world wouldn't forget what I'd done.

WALKER: Did I? How would you know that?

LUKE: I had one visit.

(*Pause.*)

WALKER: I've been through some changes. Listen Luke.
Let's begin again. I have an ex-student of mine from
Kalmytskaya visiting. Actually, it's more than that. I've
arranged for him to come. I want to help him. He's going
to need your friendship. So I'd like you to be there with
me. To welcome him. Share this new beginning with me. A
new beginning for him too.

LUKE: I could have killed him. The one I kicked.

WALKER: You could have killed him, yes. That's something
that horrified me but it's passed.

LUKE: What's your student's name? The refugee.

WALKER: Stepan. Stepan Smerdyakov. You know Natashia
was also a student of mine.

LUKE: I know!

WALKER: Of course you do. I want to make the point... that
I feel sort of involved. We are all involved. In everything.
Variously. You, me, Natashia, Stepan Smerdyakov.
(*Pause.*
NATASHIA comes on. Very agitated.)

LUKE: I didn't think you'd...

NATASHIA: I wanted to see you before tonight.

WALKER: Do you want me to go?

LUKE: Yes.

NATASHIA: No it's alright... (*To LUKE.*) This is important,
urgent. I

LUKE: You don't have to worry.

NATASHIA: I'm not worried. That's why I've come. Get it
cleared up.

LUKE: Look...

NATASHIA: Listen...

LUKE: No, look, listen, it's OK.

WALKER: I'll go to the car.

NATASHIA: You don't need to. I said already.

LUKE: Is it easier for you if he's here?

NATASHIA: Not necessarily...no...well maybe you'll listen...
take this more seriously.

LUKE: I will listen...you don't have to...

NATASHIA: You don't listen! You don't!

WALKER: Shouldn't we do this later?

LUKE: 'We?'

WALKER: You know what I mean.

LUKE: Do you know what this is about?

WALKER: Well, I know…I suspect…no, of course, yes…

NATASHIA: It's ok, you don't…I want it cleared up. (*To LUKE.*) I don't want you to be my knight in shining armour…

LUKE: Knight?

NATASHIA: You know…you know what I'm talking about.

LUKE: Yeh, I know.

WALKER: About what you did? What he did?

NATASHIA: He didn't do it for me. That's the point.

LUKE: I did it because that bastard…

NATASHIA: Listen! I once had a guy dragged me about my room by my hair saying all the time: 'I love you! Love you Nat. Natashia, I love you!' Crying. He loved me. He did love me. That guy. So he tried…

LUKE: But what's that got to do with this?

NATASHIA: He tried to find a way of SHOWING that would express what he couldn't express with words!

WALKER: I struggle with this: is what we DO the thing. In the end?

LUKE: (*To NAT.*) But you don't know why I did it!

NATASHIA: No I don't know why exactly you did it, why you beat him up…are you saying it was nothing to do with me? That's fine! Great. Let's keep it like that.

LUKE: Is anything that simple?

WALKER: We want things to be made better; that is a simple desire.

LUKE: (*To WALKER.*) You don't know what this is! You shouldn't've come!

WALKER: Look! I said I'd go!

LUKE: Yeh, I'll get a bus.

NATASHIA: It's ok. *I'm* going. I just wanted to be sure.

LUKE: You can't be sure of anything. If you want me to stay away…I'll…from you…I'll stay…but that doesn't mean the

club... He's got someone visiting...some refugee...might
like the club...

WALKER: She's not saying that.

LUKE: What?

WALKER: Not to go to the club.

LUKE: Is that right?

NATASHIA: How can I stop you? I just wanted this cleared...
if someone gets stroppy, I can deal with it.
(*Lights down.*)

Scene Three A

Ghost of LEBEDEV.

LEBEDEV: We were walking the road into our darkest night.
By moonlight. I could hear Alyosha's breathing behind
me. Ahead of me Walker talking with Grushenka. I wasn't
afraid. We weren't afraid though there may have been
snipers. Perhaps it was Walker. In that unearthly light he
seemed...like a giant. A guardian. Alyosha had once said
to me:
(*Ghost of ALYOSHA comes on.*)

ALYOSHA: Why do we need Walker? Someone like Walker?
A foreigner. Why does he want to help? What's in it for
him? And you had replied:

LEBEDEV: He cares for us. And you had said:

ALYOSHA: Do you mean, as though he loved us? In that
simple way?

LEBEDEV: And I had said: Walker told me he couldn't
separate his teaching from desiring his students. Perhaps
it's like that.

ALYOSHA: And I had said: he's a very attractive man. Very
handsome. Wonderful eyes and that mass of greying hair
swept back. One envies people like that – they seem
to have more than one life and each life is rich with
experience. He seems to be naturally loved. The soldiers
love him.

LEBEDEV: And I had said: and so he may give back that
love, yes. And you replied:

ALYOSHA: Unless it becomes just a fanciful idea and then I
  wonder whether sometimes if we indulge fanciful ideas that
  may serve our vanity, we become less alert?
LEBEDEV: And then there was the incident in Astrakhan.
  But despite that, as we walked that road to the village of
  the women, I think I loved him. Walker. Except that, now
  there was a worry: could it be that someone who lives life
  like Walker – could they with all those loves, lose focus?
  Could they be distracted from their commitment?
  (*Lights down.*)

Scene Three

NATASHIA'S room. Afternoon.

NATASHIA is rolling a joint, hands shaking. Close to breaking down.
WALKER is sitting dismayed in overcoat.

Silence.

NATASHIA: Did I seem obsessed with him?
WALKER: You're not well.
NAT.: No! Did I seem obsessed with him? Rather than
  obsessed with you?
WALKER: We must put all obsession aside. We must,
  Natashia! Obsession is bad for democracy.
NATASHIA: What?!
WALKER: I'm sorry. The war.
NATASHIA: Why have you come now? It's because Luke is
  out. You don't want me to tell him.
WALKER: Tell him. (*Short pause.*) Grace has come back. What
  we did – you and I…it's the past.
NATASHIA: A blind man – about your age, had been
  married for twenty-five years – like you. His wife
  contracted cancer. When she died he placed his hands on
  her cold face. His blind eyes filled with tears and fell on
  his now cold hands. He could see none of her death just
  as he saw nothing of her suffering. Just as he had never
  seen anything of her; the belief she had for him in her eyes
  – never saw the colour of those eyes nor the shape of those

eyes. This woman who he'd touched in her youth – felt the
breast of, put some fingers into who had admired him and
he'd never seen it; this woman who had, perhaps, been his
eyes, he now held cold in death...
(*NATASHIA stops, sniffing back tears.*)
...as though she were...a mannequin...
(*Pause.*)

WALKER: Is it me?

NATASHIA: No! It's me! I have blinded myself. Cast myself
out. Evicted myself. What judge would give a child to its
blind mother when the father is fully sighted?

WALKER: You're beautiful.

NATASHIA: Don't use platitudes! I'm suffering! I am falling!

WALKER: I'm sorry. You're right. I should know better.
Platitudes endanger us. (*Pause.*) I would like you to help.
With my student. Mr. Smerdyakov. He became involved in
that...terrible conflict: a real platitude – man's inhumanity
to man...

NATASHIA: No worse than man's inhumanity to women!

WALKER: Except it may have changed the course of history.

NATASHIA: History's what's happened and what's happened
has been subject to change. You can't change something
that's what it is because of the changes that have brought it
about! It's another cliché. Designed to excuse you for what
you shouldn't've done! From what you shouldn't have
done with me!

WALKER: There's nothing...it's not...it's me...I wanted to
see if I could CAN help you. That's why I came. Can I
help? Is there anything?

NATASHIA: Sometimes I feel...I feel I'm going...no, not
going, I feel mad. Look for solutions in arcane places. I
think...astrology, horoscopes, charts are for people who
have no one to speak to. (*Pause.*) When you taught...well
I thought you could do anything. You spoke of liberation.
You made a kind of poetry of history. Isn't that right? And
you filled me: my lungs with a rare oxygen; my mind with
the possibility of creation. And I fell into you and you
welcomed me...

(*WALKER takes NATASHIA's face in his hands. He pauses.*)
WALKER: Natashia.
(*NATASHIA suddenly begins to kiss him furiously.*
He pulls away and jumps up.)
I was wrong! I shouldn't have! I was vain! I've seen the truth! Isn't that better?
NATASHIA: No! because you've driven me towards my basest instinct! I feel as if I want revenge!
WALKER: Revenge?!
NATASHIA: I can't speak to you! I can't speak to a man who betrays his own values!
WALKER: Values! Fornication! Adultery! Have your revenge!
(*He begins to go. He stops.*)
The blind man? *C'est moi!*
(*He leaves.*)
NATASHIA: (*Shouting after him.*) Will you find redemption with your refugee? Will he comfort you?
(*Lights down.*)

Scene Four A

The Ghosts of GRUSHENKA and SONIA (speaking as if to an interviewer).

SONIA: (*To audience.*) I was studying in Drama College when the war broke out.
GRUSHENKA: We both were.
SONIA: I know that, I'm just saying... (*To audience.*) I was hoping to become an actress. What about you Grush, weren't you?... Wasn't it stage management?
GRUSHENKA: Director.
SONIA: Why're you so tetchy?
GRUSHENKA: (*To audience.*) I think what she really wanted was to go to Hollywood.
SONIA: (*To audience.*) I was ambitious. Yes.
GRUSHENKA: The point I'm making Sonia is that there's a side to you which never seems to take things that seriously – I mean film, Hollywood especially, is just not that serious while theatre...

SONIA: Wait a minute, Grush! I did fight didn't I?

GRUSHENKA: Because of me, yes. I was fighting for freedom.

SONIA: No, no, come on. It all happened so quickly who can say who fought for freedom and who didn't?

GRUSHENKA: Ok. But then we try not to think of how small the reasons for this horror…for something to have become so…big, you would expect there to be big reasons. And I just think that your way of trivialising…

SONIA: Trivialising?!

GRUSHENKA: Well…to you everything is a party.

SONIA: Now wait a minute! There's a lot that I've shut up about!

(*Silence.*)

Did Walker ever make a pass at you?

(*Pause.*)

Grush?

GRUSHENKA: I don't know. Maybe if I was in class I'd put it like that but is that the way in war? Things that happen between men and women in war seem to be beyond constraints…beyond the constraints we might put on things in a place…of study. I don't know. In a philosophical way. So he spoke to me…yes, in a way…he spoke to me in a way that you might say was making a pass.

SONIA: Was it last summer in Astrakhan? Do you remember? Lebedev brought Walker to our college. Do you remember? And do you remember how we sat in the bar and drank. And we sang and danced. And he came… he came to my room at night…

GRUSHENKA: (*Exploding.*) Yes! I remember! I remember!

SONIA: (*To audience.*) I know. I shouldn't have brought that up. It's a sore point with her. But she thinks she knows everything. Well she doesn't know what really happened with Walker!

(*Lights down.*)

Scene Four

GRACE and FRAN.

The two women are making love. They climax and fall into silence.

FRAN: What's wrong?

GRACE: George...has changed.

FRAN: So?

GRACE: He needs me.

FRAN: He's vain.

GRACE: He WAS vain.

FRAN: No. It's in the psyche just as melanin is in the skin.
There is no process that will successfully remove it.
(*GRACE laughs.*)

GRACE: Fran! How can I argue with that?

FRAN: No! Listen! Don't! Don't argue with it! George is the
student of his vanity.

GRACE: He is determined to unlearn.

FRAN: But how can he unlearn when he can't break from
his teacher? You will always find yourself at war with the
pettiness his selfishness manufactures. Whereas we, with
us, it's different! We may look at each other's eyes as Christ
looking into his mother's and though her heart is pierced,
though her tears flow, though we are torn by our realities,
we have love in the deeps of truth.

GRACE: But you're bound to say these things.

FRAN: Why do you say that? As though you can qualify my
feelings and then...I don't know...slide out from beneath
them. We don't do this lightly.

GRACE: You don't have to tell me, Fran! None of this is done
on a whim. How could it be? For me.

FRAN: Then just understand that NOTHING is more
important to me than this. It's as though it was born in
pre-history; as though all my antecedents existed for me to
be here NOW or at any one of those nows with you. Your
husband may be one of the most wonderful men who ever
lived but not for you because he is borne on a pulse of
narrative from which he disappears only to reappear: like

he was in a small boat on a fast running river and when
he gets into difficulty, strange arms will stretch out from
the bank to save him. And he will fall into them like the
wounded into a hospital bed.

(*They kiss.*)

GRACE: Stop! I can't. Luke is home. We have come together
again. A family.

(*They kiss.*

Lights down.)

THE GHOSTS: (*In the darkness.*) In my death
I remember the days
When my grandfather's grandfather sold ribbons in Baku.

Scene Five

The same. Early evening.

LUKE is sitting. NATASHIA is smoking.

LUKE: That guy. The one. The one I went down for. D'you
ever see him?

NATASHIA: No.

LUKE: Not since that night?

NATASHIA: Probably not. It would have taken him a long
time to recover.

LUKE: He deserved it.

NATASHIA: It was my fault.

LUKE: He called you a cunt.

NATASHIA: I wound him up. I was annoyed.

LUKE: About what?

NATASHIA: The man I loved left me. Ditched me.

LUKE: Ditched YOU? And it made you angry?

NATASHIA: Yes. I was upset.

LUKE: Not angry.

NATASHIA: Angry, upset, what…

LUKE: No…listen…if you were upset you'd be different.
From what you'd be if you were angry. He shouted. From
the audience. You were upset and answered him then HE
got angry. He got angry.

NATASHIA: My songs are angry.

LUKE: Your songs are angry but that doesn't mean you're always angry! Anyway, if he's getting angry because your songs are angry what kind of fascist is that? As far as I'm concerned that kind of person is scum because he wants everybody to be sitting around smiling all day long and we don't live in that kind of world. Well...we do actually live in the kind of world where people don't want us to be angry but it's the kind of world which should make us want to be angry and we should defend our right to be angry at all cost. Whatever it cost. We mustn't ever be afraid to be angry; never let any bastard ever tell us you CAN'T BE ANGRY especially when they're the ones getting angry telling us! That's the category he falls into. He's a nihilist. I hate that shit.

(*Silence.*)

NATASHIA: You should help your father with his refugee. Befriend the refugee. Help your father with his book. You should do this. Avoid obsessions. Help the refugee.

(*Pause.*)

LUKE: He is coming.

NATASHIA: What?

LUKE: He is coming. From out of the East.

NATASHIA: Befriend him. He'll need you. He's ill. He has an illness. Fits. Blackouts.

LUKE: Fits.

NATASHIA: Maybe not. This isn't a war zone.

(*Pause.*)

Go now.

LUKE: Go?

NATASHIA: I want something left.

LUKE: You mean you don't want to use up all your patience. That's what you mean. Don't go to prison. That's all I can say to you. Don't go to prison if you're going to use up all your patience in a few minutes.

NATASHIA: I'm not going to prison.

LUKE: You don't really know. No one can tell. The world's full of fascists and nihilists. People with fat guts in woolly pullovers. These are the worst. The decent amongst us. Abusing language. Telling any lie to get power. The historians and the philosophers pave the way. The politicians follow.

NATASHIA: It's time to leave.

LUKE: I know about time.

NATASHIA: Not now.

LUKE: Now is not the right time to talk about time?! I've had time, time like snowdrifts up to my neck in snow and time! You throw time away! Everyone! Throw other people's time away...the nihilists they deface time: it's unrecognisable! 1914, 1918, 1939, 1945 – this is time: DATES! We all serve this time! You think only I served time...think about that – served time; what were the dates of my time? DOESN'T EXIST! I served nothing! I served the absence of time. And you – were you having a good time? Were you just passing time? How can we pass time? Is time something you pass on the street? Time passed me by – during the time of my incarceration I was timeless – was I eternal? If I was not eternal I was nothing – in neither case did I serve time unless...unless waiting to see you again was serving something...maybe time that you embodied that you probably SQUANDERED!

NATASHIA: (*Jumping up.*) Get out! Get out!

(*Lights down.*)

Scene Six

WALKER's. Afternoon.

WALKER a little agitated. SMERDYAKOV alert.

SMERDYAKOV: I am sorry. Professor Walker. I am stupid.

WALKER: Don't call me Professor, Stepan. George. As it was out there. Call me George.

SMERDYAKOV: I do not know what it is you want me to say.

WALKER: I don't want you to say anything. Well...I suppose what I mean is I certainly wouldn't want to direct you in saying anything. We'll meet later. Have a chat later.

Tomorrow. That'll be something to look forward to. (*Pause.*)
Are you well?

SMERDYAKOV: I am quite well.

WALKER: What about your illness? Are you still suffering…?
Do you still have… You're sweating. Here, let me.
(*WALKER wipes SMERDYAKOV's brow.*)

SMERDYAKOV: I think…I am hoping that things will be
better. Here.

WALKER: Things will be better here, I'm sure.

SMERDYAKOV: I think it was the war.

WALKER: The circumstances of the war, of course, would
have exacerbated things.

SMERDYAKOV: Well there is something I need…I need
badly…to talk about.

WALKER: Later. We'll talk later, of course. You see, now is a
difficult time as we're expecting Luke. My son.

SMERDYAKOV: I never knew about him. Before. About
your son.

WALKER: No. I dare say…well, it's quite likely I never
mentioned him. Over there. Things were different.

SMERDYAKOV: I think I see that.

WALKER: You do?

SMERDYAKOV: Yes, well…I felt immediately on my arrival
that you were different. Different from out there.

WALKER: 'Different from…', you remember that. Not
different *to* or different *than* as the Americans say.

SMERDYAKOV: I remember everything you taught me.
I remember these feelings. All those feelings. Honour. I
remember feeling the honour. Of being your student. I
remember how I would feel in the morning – in the days
just before the war. The days of excitement. That we would
make history. Those were the best days for me. Before the
war. The days of the war. They were different. They were
the most important days. Of my life. Because of you.

WALKER: I'm pleased you feel that Stepan. It encourages me.
Of course, things are different now. I'm bound to see things
differently now. History.

SMERDYAKOV: I know. Well I think I feel that. This is a
new feeling. This is something...

WALKER: Something we can talk about later.

(*LUKE comes on.*
He stands in silence for a brief moment appraising SMERDYAKOV
with something like wonder.
The two look at him.)

LUKE: This is him then. The refugee. Stepan Smerdyakov.
I've practised the name. The warrior. My father's student.
Hopefully my friend. I hope you'll be my friend. Look at
him! It's a miracle! I've been away and now I'm home. (*To
WALKER.*) Does Mr...does Stepan. (*To SMERDYAKOV.*)
you don't mind me being friendly do you? (*To WALKER.*)
Does he know where I've been?

WALKER: My son...Luke fell foul of the authorities.

LUKE: 'Fell foul of the authorities'...excellent! I was trying to
think of how to introduce myself...what to speak about...
how to break the ice. (*Pause.*) Have you heard, Stepan, of
the fifty-seven varieties?

SMERDYAKOV: I am sorry...

LUKE: God! Don't be sorry! Heinz fifty-seven varieties!
Where I was, that was the kind of thing you'd turn your
mind to; the kind of thing you contemplate is the fifty-
seven varieties: what are they? In there I had a friend
– from your neck of the woods – a Romanian. We called
him Brutalescu, a refugee a little like yourself – or so he
claimed. With Brutalescu we identified fifty-one varieties.
It's a good way into friendship. We could do it sometime if
you like.

SMERDYAKOV: I would like that.

LUKE: Good response! We're going to be good friends! The
best!

WALKER: I wouldn't mind finding that out myself! The fifty-
seven varieties!

LUKE: Have you told him about the club?

WALKER: Haven't really had the opportunity...

LUKE: Well, there's this club we go to. A friend of ours – a
young woman who is very beautiful so eyes off, ha, ha!,
Natashia sings there.

WALKER: It was there the incident happened.

(*Pause.*)

LUKE: That's strange! That you should say that! That you should tell him that... (*Pause.*) Never mind. It was but a rare event – it's not a brawler's paradise – not even any bouncers. She sings deep, sort of political songs so you don't get the bruisers in except on this one very rare occasion – I had to deal with it. Turns out he was a judge's son, kind of lager lout hooray henry – my bad luck. I only tapped him...

WALKER: Luke doesn't really know his own strength.

(*Pause.*)

LUKE: Again! A strange thing to say! (*Short pause.*) I just felt I had to defend her – we're not talking here about a new age of chivalry nor 'don't mess with my babe'...just common decency – let the flower bloom; don't let the drunks piss on the roses or trample the grass – there's too much of that. To be honest, inside, one of the things that would wind us up more than anything was reflecting on the trash in civvy street – the loutish behaviour of the drunken burger munchers and coke swillers oblivious of the fact that, for example, Coca Cola funds death squads in Colombia – she told me that, Natashia who you will meet this evening I take it that's where we're going?

WALKER: Yes.

LUKE: Then that's where we'll go! And here's Grace. How neat!

(*LUKE leaves.*

GRACE comes on.)

WALKER: Grace, this is Stepan.

GRACE: O my God. I'm so pleased to meet you. Stepan.

(*SMERDYAKOV stands shakily. They shake hands.*)

It's in the handshake.

WALKER: What? What is Grace?

GRACE: All the fragility of...us. You and me.

SMERDYAKOV: I am sorry. The flight affected me. I am cold.

WALKER: That's tiredness.

GRACE: It's as if you've been ambushed.

SMERDYAKOV: And do you feel that?

GRACE: Do you mean do I feel it coming from you?

SMERDYAKOV: I meant: do you know this feeling?

(*Pause.*)

WALKER: Well I don't think...

GRACE: No. I do. I do know it. I must. I suppose. I said the word.

WALKER: Look at the effect you have on people, Stepan. Like a visitor from a Russian novel! Ha, ha!

GRACE: No, no, George. I do know it. But I'm prepared to think that it's...that it's because I was worried about you. Out there. For now. It's good to meet you Stepan. One word. Ambush. Strange. It can open up...I don't know... what's been closed. I suppose. Let's meet later. Again. (*GRACE leaves thoughtful.*)

SMERDYAKOV: Yes. I would like that. (*Pause* *SMERDYAKOV and WALKER look at each other. They look as if they are about to embrace.*) I lost...lost belief.

WALKER: You'll feel better tomorrow.

SMERDYAKOV: We did not only lose our lives. We lost so much more

WALKER: We didn't lose our lives! (*Lights down.*)

Scene Seven A

Ghosts of LEBEDEV and ALYOSHA.

LEBEDEV: We came over the crest of a hill. Alyosha and me had fallen back. The moon was full and lit the village with an eerie, unsettling light. At that point we were unafraid. There is something about that light; that moonlight: it's almost ironic. Like looking into a mirror and seeing beyond the reflection. And then, there was a moment when Walker seemed to swagger! And suddenly, in that moonlight with that thought about the mirror, his swagger

allowed me to question something he had said. And I said
to Alyosha: what do you think Walker meant when he said
'we haven't finished creating YOUR history'? And you
said:

ALYOSHA: He was urging us on.

LEBEDEV: But is our history different from his? Is it
something in the end he creates? Despotically? If so, why
have we allowed him this power? And I couldn't believe it
when you said:

ALYOSHA: It's an academic point.

LEBEDEV: And I said: no! We've given him this power
because of belief. We believed in him because he is driven
by belief.

ALYOSHA: And I said: yes! He believes in our cause!

LEBEDEV: And I said: but these things aren't a matter
of belief! History is the reconciliation of opposites: it's
scientific; it's mathematics – it's beauty! Why is Walker
here? He doesn't believe this! He believes in Michelet! In
Michelet there is no reconciliation!

ALYOSHA: This is where you flicked my cross as though it
were nothing more than the tin it was made of.

LEBEDEV: I was drawing attention to this: that belief in
the way you believe is self-sufficient. It doesn't need
justification which means all can be justified!...

ALYOSHA: It is sufficient...

LEBEDEV: And this is the way it is with Walker so that
he may say I believe this and I believe that! *I* believe. I
believe that whatever we do is right. I believe that any
expression of anger is justified in this context. Don't you
see: everything may be reduced to HIS belief. But belief
is meaningless. His belief becomes his history. Look down
there Alyosha. Look into the valley! Look at the village.
What do you see?

ALYOSHA: And I said: nothing. Only a village in the
moonlight. It's peaceful.

LEBEDEV: And I said: Impossible! We're looking beyond the
mirror's reflection!

ALYOSHA: And then I said: what are you getting at?

33

LEBEDEV: And I said: look at them; look at how he walks with Grushenka and look at Sonia, behind. How she walks behind, head hanging down. And I said: Do you know what happened in Astrakhan? Between Walker and Sonia. We overlooked it at the time.

ALYOSHA: And I said: he'd been drinking. He was a little drunk. It was nothing. And, I said: if we overlooked it then why are we not overlooking it now? And if it had hurt her why did she give no sign of it in Walker's presence?

LEBEDEV: And I said: because she was a soldier!

ALYOSHA: And I said: Well, if that was the case, then Walker would have been much less important than you think he was. A man in whom reputation is a posture.
(*Lights down.*)

Scene Seven

Nightclub. Low lighting. Early evening. (Music?.)

LUKE and SMERDYAKOV.

LUKE: In your country. There's a lot of death. Isn't there?

SMERDYAKOV: I am sorry? I think I am stupid.

LUKE: No. Isn't that why you left? So you would have a more acute understanding upon reflection. I mean, everyone is riveted by death. A man kills fifteen children over a period of years and then gets caught. What we want is to know the detail. How their poor little bodies were thrown into rivers and down railway embankments after he'd slit them open. After he'd raped them. Details! Then hang him.

SMERDYAKOV: You want to talk about murder?

LUKE: The living in your country are counting their dead like old men at their cribbage! Killing, murder…tell me about the killing in your country.

SMERDYAKOV: There is a war.

LUKE: But what's the difference? You get a bullet in the head, you get a bullet in the head! Doesn't matter whether it's Mafia or the army.

SMERDYAKOV: Are you asking was I…I myself involved, did I witness any…

LUKE: Let me tell you what I think I'm getting at. See if you agree. I believe that in your country, murder has become an act of reassurance.

(*Silence.*)

That's interesting! You've gone completely silent. You should see your eyes! Right now! You should…it's Brutalescu all over again. Wouldn't you agree…wouldn't you think it's true that when someone murders another – or, if we're going to split hairs, KILLS another – that they demystify death and that that gives them some control over it? Over death. And the horror of the unknown – nothingness, is made less.

(*Silence.*

WALKER comes on with drinks.

FRAN is with him.)

WALKER: Luke. Let me introduce you to Fran. She's a friend of your mother's. I found her at the bar!

LUKE: Hello Fran. She's not really my mother.

FRAN: She told me about your trouble. Is everything alright now?

LUKE: Yes. Everything is fine. This is Mr Smerdyakov, our refugee!

WALKER: You don't have to put it quite like that!

LUKE: (*To FRAN.*) He's been ill. I'm curing him!

WALKER: (*To FRAN.*) I've asked him to look after Stepan for me. Would you like to join us?

FRAN: It's ok. Thanks. I have to go.

(*She leaves.*)

LUKE: Goodbye Fran.

FRAN: (*Stopping and turning back to face LUKE.*) This man is falling.

(*Silence.*

FRAN leaves.)

WALKER: I haven't told you, have I Luke, that I'm writing a book…I mean, I've written books before but this, this is not ANY book…

SMERDYAKOV: Professor Walker wrote such a book about our country. It was very influential.

LUKE: A book? That's fascinating. A book. I'd really like to help if I could. That would be good for me. Maybe get acknowledged.

WALKER: Well perhaps you could listen to what I have to say because that would be a great help to me. I am asking: what is the truth of conflict? We know that the victors write the history. But the real history is told at a much more profound, personal level. The real story takes place in the shadows of rooms; in the secrets held by people whose main drive may be love. (*Pause.*) What do you think, Stepan? Do you think what I'm saying is unnerving for you? Given that what I taught you is almost diametrically opposed...

LUKE: I like this. I'm intrigued by this. Are there such stories? Stepan?

(*Pause.*)

SMERDYAKOV: Memory is strange. Sometimes it drives you to explore the truth. Sometimes...to save yourself.

LUKE: That's very mysterious. Isn't it?

(*Pause.*)

WALKER: I think...I think we have to stop the history of facts. History should become more emotional. We need to recognise the power of film and fiction and metaphor and let that be our motivation.

LUKE: Inside, I saw a film. A Hollywood film. A film made in the thirties. In it an English spy pretending to be a Bolshevik has to take a princess to a town where, presumably, she will be executed. He kisses her. It's not his intention. That's the power of it. As a result of the kiss, things change. History changes. Is that what you're talking about?

WALKER: Well...yes. It could be. What was the film?

LUKE: Don't know. Anyway, I wouldn't put much on it. A kiss won't change history. Sex will. Wouldn't you say Stepan? Wouldn't you say that your war was about sex? Driven by it? All your leaders will have lots of sex won't they? Ours do.

SMERDYAKOV: (*To WALKER.*) Does it help you...in your soul...does it help you to begin your history from now? From this moment?

LUKE: Why don't you answer, Stepan? A man from your country goes to war in the circumstances of the war in your country and he's going for sex. I think I believe that. Yes. He anticipates the hot nights in some rural backwater where the young women will be obliged to give him what he wants! God, I can smell it myself!

SMERDYAKOV: I am sorry. I am not familiar with this. Perhaps it is your fantasy.

WALKER: The long nights of your incarceration could produce these thoughts.

LUKE: No! A village is a woman; a country is a woman! And an army is a man intent on rape!

SMERDYAKOV: But this is your way of seeing the world. Your army. Your country.

LUKE: I've seen it on TV! I've seen the men from your country going to war and they LOOK as if they're going to war to rape! Definitely not to kiss!

SMERDYAKOV: But how would you know what a man who sets out in the morning to rape looks like? All you know about these men you have seen is that they are going to fight a war!

LUKE: And by the end of the day he's raped half a village! The proof of the pudding! It's human nature. European nihilism!

SMERDYAKOV: I do not know what you mean.

WALKER: No, enough, Luke! You're getting Stepan excited! It's not good... (*He looks off.*) Let's change...here's Natashia.

LUKE: Nietzsche! He foresaw the nihilism that would embrace Europe! Democracy. It's anti-democratic! The rule of the weak over the strong. Most people are fools, clowns. In your country the strong are reasserting themselves....

(*NATASHIA comes on. SMERDYAKOV looks at her intensely.*)

...But they have to practise. Rape! Rape is the practising of strength!

(*NATASHIA stands in silence looking intensely at LUKE for an instamt.*)

You overheard that. Not something I'm advocating...we were discussing...well...morality – the morality or otherwise of warfare.

(*NATASHIA looks at SMERDYAKOV and takes a step backwards as if overwhelmed by something.*)

...it's useful to discuss these things. This is...

WALKER: This is our refugee. Stepan Smerdyakov. Stepan, Natashia.

(*SMERDYAKOV gets up holding his hand out. He seems awestruck by NATASHIA – almost a moment of recognition.*

They shake hands.

Silence.

SMERDYAKOV sits.

NATASHIA is about to say something then turns and walks away.)

LUKE: (*Calling after her.*) Natashia, wait! I've got something for you.

WALKER: Luke, not now. I wouldn't.

LUKE: You wouldn't? Wouldn't what?

WALKER: I think the moment...was difficult for her...

SMERDYAKOV: She is beautiful.

LUKE: Well that's the first sensible thing you've said all night! It's true!

WALKER: I'm going now. Stepan...it would be good...I think, later, perhaps, or tomorrow morning, if we could have a chat. The two of us.

SMERDYAKOV: Should I come now?

LUKE: No! You haven't heard her sing yet. You've got to hear her sing.

WALKER: It's alright. You stay. I need to go. Now.

(*Lights down.*)

Scene Eight A

Ghost of LEBEDEV.

LEBEDEV: *The Brothers Karamazov.* Dostoievsky. And there is
in that novel the character Smerdyakov. A lackey. A kind
of lumpen being. The distorted reflection of the powerful
ideas of his legitimate brother Ivan. It's the mirror again.
But what about OUR Smerdyakov? Had he gone beyond
the mirror? As we came across first sight of the army
bivouacked outside the village so that they couldn't be
seen from the hill despite the moonlight, and as we became
aware of the moaning, Alyosha said – as though reading
my thoughts:
(Ghost of ALYOSHA comes on.)
ALYOSHA: Perhaps Smerdyakov is the key to Walker.
LEBEDEV: And I said: I don't understand.
ALYOSHA: And I said: the soldiers are here. Something has
happened. You can hear it. Will Smerdyakov's respect for
beauty make Walker just?
LEBEDEV: And I said: perhaps. Unless Smerdyakov is
corrupted by Walker's reputation.
(Lights down.)

Scene Eight

The same. Later. Late evening.

LUKE and SMERDYAKOV. The sound of applause.

LUKE: *(A little drunk.)* What's going on Stepan? What's going
on in our world – your world, my world – what is your
world? European? Asian? I don't know, does it matter?
What's going on in our world? The people with the soul
are the terrorists. That's crazy! I could be a terrorist
because I so desperately want meaning, but look what I
got to do to get it. I know what the terrorist is like; what
he thinks, what he feels, how he wakes up in the middle
of the night in a cold sweat, looks at his world dominated
by the profit barons who have no country driven by it

doesn't matter what – sell it, cheap shit, you name it and
he can see all his people, he's losing them, they're sinking
into the sand, they can't see it, they think they're having a
good time; they think this is what they want and he's losing
them and all his people are going and there's nothing he
can do. He wants to be somebody, not somebody great just
somebody in his own community, in his own village, in
his own town – he wants everybody else to be somebody
too; he doesn't want to be a somebody amongst a whole
load of people who just want to, you know, lay down and
take it. You know what frightens me most? What most
frightens me? I can't seem to control my anger, my anger
at the world. I may become a terrorist. Terrorism is only
beginning. Now. In its infancy. You'll either be a slave to
some corporation or a terrorist. Corporatism or terrorism.
That's the only choice. That's coming. The terrorists are
the moralists. It's easy to do it. Once you've crossed that
line. Easy. Hey Natashia! Come here. Come over here.
She's coming.

SMERDYAKOV: She's beautiful.

LUKE: Hands off, she's mine! Ha, ha. Watch this.

(*NATASHIA comes to table and stands by it in silence.*)

(*To NATASHIA.*) You know I said I had something for you?

(*LUKE takes out a small box and hands it to her.*)

NATAЗHIA: Why did you bring him here?

LUKE: We wanted to show him the real thing. You.

NATASHIA: I'm not the real thing. (*Pause.*) He is.

(*Short pause.*)

LUKE: So are those. Gold.

(*NATASHIA takes out a pair of earrings.*)

SMERDYAKOV: Your songs are very powerful. Very moving.
I understand them.

NATASHIA: This man makes me nervous.

SMERDYAKOV: I am sorry.

LUKE: He needn't.

NATASHIA: You think he's a fool.

LUKE: Not me!

NATASHIA: I don't want these.

(*She hands earrings back to LUKE.*)

LUKE: But why? Why not. You don't want to take them in front of him...is that it? Come on Nat. Take them!

NATASHIA: No!

LUKE: Alright. Not today. Tomorrow? What if he's with me? (*Aside to her.*) Natashia, I'd do anything for you!

NATASHIA: Would you? Climb any mountain? Swim any river? Sail any sea? Cross any desert? Fight any war? Kill any rival? Would you scale any wall or shin any pole? Would you give me the stars or all the world's Demerara? (*NATASHIA goes.*)

SMERDYAKOV: She is more beautiful than I thought. She is suffering.

LUKE: It's fashionable. Designer suffering. SHE'S fashionable.

SMERDYAKOV: She has lost something.

LUKE: Lost! Hey, we are all lost! Listen. I know what this is. She looks at you and she sees suffering and you will want to milk that sympathy of hers. Well don't.

SMERDYAKOV: I am sorry. I do not...

LUKE: I suppose you think she put me down?

SMERDYAKOV: I do not know. But I understand what she feels. She is living the life her songs condemn. And you have brought me into her nightclub. Somebody who has just come from where the suffering she makes the song of, is going on. Not only that, but you bring her this gift. As though her love for you could be so small. So cheap.

LUKE: Cheap!

SMERDYAKOV: She feels guilty because I am here. That is why she gave back the earrings. That is why she said what she said. You are good. You meant well but did the wrong thing. I have pity for you. I do not think you have ever made love with that woman.
(*Pause.*)

LUKE: Let me tell you this, between you and me, you bloody Slav, that's just a bit of wishful thinking. Just keep your greasy hands off her!
(*Both men look shocked.*)

Sorry! Don't know why I said that. You must have driven
me to it.

SMERDYAKOV: I am sorry. I made you angry.

LUKE: I'm a driven man. It's a sense. (*Short pause.*) I think it's
a sense of catastrophe. As though I'm…not being driven
on but forced to run away.

SMERDYAKOV: No. You live at the heart of chaos and you
are desperate to replace it with a bourgeois comfort and
order.

LUKE: Bourgeois!

SMERDYAKOV: I am sorry. Perhaps it is the wrong word.

LUKE: You would know all about chaos but you know
nothing about me! (*Pause.*) After the sexual murders of
his victims, the killer spoke: he remembered his crimes
as metaphysical episodes in which the victims become
his brides. After twenty or thirty the experience becomes
the same because you are the LAST ONE THERE! You
FEEL the last bit of breath leaving their body just as you
come! Is this, do you think, a psychological profile of a
killer in the West or in your war? Who is it, for example,
going into villages and raping and murdering – looking
into the eyes as the last breath is breathed and the come
enters the fading body – with the intention of making that
village, that land, THEIRS?
(*Silence.*)
Come on, Stepan! (*Viciously.*) To you lot murder is a kind
of democracy let alone metaphysic! Isn't THAT true?
Because you're all nihilists! You've embraced this war
that's killed so many and driven a stake into the heart of
meaning and now you don't want to talk about it! As if it
never happened!

SMERDYAKOV: (*Close to tears.*) I would gladly die myself
if it could show that these murders, our murders, are not
simply evil. If you want me to talk about it, I will talk
about it! (*Pause.*) There was such a murder as your kind in
our town. But it was like this: (*Pause.*) Two elderly working
men had come to a clandestine religious meeting and were
staying overnight. They were sharing the same bedroom.

One of the men owned a cross that the other became passionate for.

LUKE: A cross?

SMERDYAKOV: Yes. Like you would wear around your neck. While the man with the cross slept the other said a prayer of forgiveness and then slit his throat. He stole the cross and got away. That is the condition of your kind of murder in our country.

LUKE: Was he found?

SMERDYAKOV: No.

LUKE: Then how'd you know about it?... Shit, go on!

SMERDYAKOV: Some days later I saw a drunk on the street. He seemed tormented by more than just drink. As I passed he held out his hand. In it was a cross: 'Buy my cross sir! It is all I have left but breath. Save me.' The cross was obviously made of tin. You can buy one like it in any bazaar. I bought it.

LUKE: It was the cross! The cross of the murdered man. Wasn't it? That's why you bought it. You knew! But how could you have known? Did you have inside info?

SMERDYAKOV: I bought it to...to own despair. (*Pause.*) They are burning books to cook the bread. They are destroying history for a few more moments of life. That cross was a symbol of the despair everywhere. It could have been the murder cross. I was afraid of it. I had to own it like murderers own death.

LUKE: You're holding something back! You knew that it WAS the cross! Christ, I love that story! It's one of the best stories I've ever heard! (*Pause.*) Stepan?

SMERDYAKOV: Yes?

LUKE: I'm...I'm sorry...sorry for my manner. (*Pause.*) Have you got it? With you? I'll give you anything for it.

SMERDYAKOV: But why?

LUKE: Isn't it obvious? A tin cross. The symbol of Christ's passion. One man is killed for it; you are driven to despair by it! You bought it to own despair! Nothing could be more valuable! I want the cross! Forget everything I said,

Stepan…if I insulted you: all of it – it's nothing. Please. I
must have the cross. What's the matter? You've gone white!
(*SMERDYAKOV'S head crashes to the table.*)
LUKE: Christ! Natashia! Natashia!
(*Lights down.*)

Scene Nine

Natashia's Room. Mid-day.

*NATASHIA is sketching (a sketch of SMERDYAKOV's eyes). LUKE
comes on.*

LUKE: No funny stuff, Nat. Honest. Just wanted to say thanks
for helping me with Stepan. He's resting but I think it's
terminal.
NATASHIA: What?!
LUKE: Look how that bothers you! Why? Why should it?
We're all terminal cases but why should it bother you
so much that that Cossack – whatever he is – should be,
maybe, a bit more terminal than us?
(*Silence.*)
See? Silence. I know I shouldn't have tried to give you
those earrings…I'm sorry…if I ever tried anything like that
again…
NATASHIA: Don't!
LUKE: No! Listen. If I ever it would be with something that
money couldn't buy.
NATASHIA: I don't want ANYTHING!
LUKE: No. It's ok. Forget it. I'm on your side. Except, in here
it's different. Isn't it?
(*He takes out earrings.*)
No one can see. Take them, Nat. Please.
(*She looks at him in silence.*)
He holds earrings clumsily.
NATASHIA: Where is he?
LUKE: In his room. What you drawing? Can I have a look?
(*He looks at NATASHIA's sketch.*)
Eyes. Just for a second, almost without thinking as my
head turned and my eye caught the light from the lamp

I thought they were my father's. His eyes. But now I can
see they're Stepan's. I know his eyes. I've looked right into
them. Like some deep Siberian lake. (*Pause.*) I won't ask
you why you sketched HIS eyes.

NATASHIA: It's nothing, ok? I was doodling. That's all. I
don't love him. I don't love you. I don't love anyone.

LUKE: That's not true. You love your son.

NATASHIA: What do you know about my son?

LUKE: I know you had a son. My father told me. Was it him?
The father.

NATASHIA: Who?!

LUKE: The one who called you a cunt! The one I did time
for. Because I would feel o so proud if I'd dealt a blow to
the vanity of such a bastard who could think he is so SO
good, so, you know – hey, I'm the king dude – to do that
to you.

NATASHIA: It wasn't him.

(*LUKE offers the earrings again.*)

LUKE: Nat?

NATASHIA: Jesus! Jesus! I don't want them!

(*Silence.*

LUKE turns away and puts earrings in his pocket.)

LUKE: Now I think of it, if it was your son you loved, were
missing, you'd be sketching HIS eyes, not the eyes of
a stranger. I can't bear this because I know all you're
thinking about is Stepan. I saw how you looked at him.

NATASHIA: No! Listen! Don't be a fool. I looked into his face
and I could see that thing – that knowledge that only those
who have suffered the exploding shells and flying blood
of other people carry with them. A man stripped naked
by the explosions! It's a knowledge that those who create
wars can never experience and it lets those who see look
into the soul of mystery and nothing NOTHING is ever
again mysterious! Nothing is ever again mysterious! That is
shocking!

(*Lights down.*)

Scene Ten A

Ghost of LEBEDEV.

LEBEDEV: That night, that final night, as we sat with the soldiers I asked Walker what he knew about Chechnya and what he thought about it; about what he knew. He said: 'tell me. You tell me. Tell me all about Chechnya.' So I did (*Pause.*) And then, as I finished, he said to me: 'I'd like you to tell me what YOU think' – as though he wasn't sure what might be the right – or wrong – thing to say. Except it wasn't that. He was playing with me. He was toying with me and it became part of the camaraderie he shared with the soldiers. It became clear that his relationship with them was one in which they flattered him and that it wasn't so much that they would do anything for him but that he would never fail to support them in whatever it was they would do.
(*Lights down.*)

Scene Ten

GRACE and FRAN.

The two women are kissing.

GRACE: We'll have to stop!
FRAN: Why?
GRACE: I told you! I've gone back to George.
FRAN: But why?
GRACE: Because he's my husband.
FRAN: He's a man. Doesn't believe in you. Believes in only one thing: himself.
GRACE: No. He's changed.
FRAN: How?
GRACE: This war.
FRAN: No! How?
GRACE: He's shown humility. Understanding.
FRAN: He's vain.
GRACE: He admits that! He knows that!

FRAN: He wants something or he's hiding something. We are in love.

GRACE: We were never in love. It was the sex. It was like an impossible freedom. Because some freedom is impossible.

FRAN: You can't betray your feelings. If you can do that, there's nothing.

GRACE: Stop it Fran! This is hurting!

FRAN: There is either us and the universe or there is that small man you want to serve. A petty TV celebrity.

GRACE: Don't talk about him like that. He's rejected it. He's not the same. He knows how none of that means anything.

FRAN: But you don't.

GRACE: What?

FRAN: What's he offered you? What's he buying you with? He can't offer you what I can – the deepest pounding of my heart. You misunderstand. There is something so tired and worn about that convention you want to share with him. It has no challenge. Become too safe. Bourgeois. Without purpose. To defend it, any inhumanity may be visited on anyone. Do you want your centre to crumble? Do you want anarchy in your dreams? Do you want your world to become a raging battlefield of maleness?

GRACE: Just leave me. Leave me, Fran.

FRAN: I can't carry on like this! Picking you up after every fall. One day you'll fall and I'll leave you!

(*Silence.*)

Listen. I saw them. Your family. With the refugee who's staying with you. Ask yourself: what's going on there? George has asked Luke to look after the refugee. The poor man is ill and he is NURSED by Luke? What's George up to?

(*GRACE walks away.*

Lights down.)

THE GHOSTS: (*In the darkness.*) In my death

I remember the days

When my grandfather's grandfather sold ribbons in Baku.

Scene Eleven

Smerdyakov's room. A bed. Evening.

SMERDYAKOV is in bed sleeping. LUKE comes on carrying a tray with soup and a French roll.

He quietly puts the tray down and begins frantically but quietly to search (for the cross).

After a moment, SMERDYAKOV wakes.

LUKE: (*Cheerfully.*) I owe you an apology, Stepan. I had no idea that the war in your country had taken such a toll on you.
(*Silence.*)
I didn't know anyone could look so dead and not be! I've brought you some soup.
(*Silence.*)
I'm surprised at how shy you are when we talk about killing. One would have expected that you'd got over the embarrassment. But then, I would think that wouldn't I? These things in your country have such a high profile in ours. Do you want me to help you with this soup?
(*As he speaks, LUKE props SMERDYAKOV up against his pillow and feeds him his soup. He handles him gently.*)
If murder could enable us to kill our own personal deaths, how many do you think would NOT kill? Not many! O yes, there's a murderer in each and every one of us.
(*Silence.*)
Take your two men and their cross. Let's imagine it was like this: it's night. Neither is drunk. In fact, both are old. One has this common, not exactly common, PROSAIC cross. For no reason that anyone in the world can fathom, the one rises up out of his bed, takes out...the knife! Where would he have got the knife? Had he come prepared? Did he leave the room? Sneak down to the hotel kitchen? Pick up a chef's large knife? Creep back up the stairs on tiptoe....

SMERDYAKOV: He was a working man. He worked with a knife.

LUKE: You know this? OK. So, he rose up out of his bed, stole across the room, slit the throat of the man in the other bed – his NEIGHBOUR, perhaps! – and, O, so very carefully, DEFTLY, lifted from around his neck, this cheap, tin cross. (*Pause.*) Did it have ANYTHING to do with the war we know about?

(*Silence.*)

If it did then the murder would be meaningless! And the cross – well, just something that happened to be there. But that cross cost a man his life and that's what gives it its worth. Its value. Agree?

SMERDYAKOV: (*Feverishly.*) You have brought soup to a sick man. When you are ill, the sense of taste goes. You bring me the soup and you say it is good. Tasty. With WORTH. But to me it tastes awful because I am ill. So is it good or not? Worthy or not? If you say it is good, should I trust you? The food may be bad. You may be poisoning me. Its worth may be in its ability to kill me. It is the same with men. I bring you a man – Judas. I say he is your friend. He kisses you and smiles. Two days later you are dead with a knife in your back.

LUKE: Are you saying you don't trust me? No! You're saying that you do! Good is more than a matter of taste.

(*Pause.*

LUKE holds SMERDYAKOV tenderly.)

Stepan, I'm sorry. I get angry but I don't mean to. I just feel…I feel I'm getting close to something. With the cross.

(*LUKE hugs SMERDYAKOV.*)

Eat.

(*SMERDYAKOV eats soup from spoon LUKE offers.*)

Listen! The value that that cross has is a worth that no golden trinket could ever possess. And this is the most important thing to me. Of all the deaths in your country, THIS is the only one that means anything! It's the only one with imagination; the only CREATIVE one! It's the only democratic death!

(*Silence.*)
Of all the people you've met since you arrived here, just
tell me, which one do you think would most appreciate
such a cross? Which one?
(*Silence.*)
Come on! I know you know what I'm getting at!
(*Pause.*)

SMERDYAKOV: No.

LUKE: What?

SMERDYAKOV: No.

LUKE: No? (*Pause.*) How can you say no? How much do you
want for it? Fifty? A hundred quid? What's your price? Just
name it. Anything! I want that cross!

SMERDYAKOV: No!

(*LUKE jumps up.*)

LUKE: Suddenly you're an idiot?! What is it? Come on! I
meant it Stepan! I've pissed around enough! Tell me!

SMERDYAKOV: No.

LUKE: 'No'! 'Yes'! These are the words of a spy! A terrorist!
A man under interrogation! All I'm asking for is a piece of
tin!

(*LUKE picks up the French loaf and raises it as if to hit
SMERDYAKOV across the head with it.*)

Where is it?!

SMERDYAKOV: (*Suddenly feverishly.*) A piece of tin! Yes!
Nothing! It is nothing! Only something because of
your obsession! Only your obsession that is making
it something! It is nothing! Nothing! I have come to a
country of nothingness! Obsessions! It is.

(*LUKE suddenly stuffs the loaf into SMERDYAKOV's mouth.
SMERDYAKOV is now convulsing. LUKE immediately sets
about searching for the cross again. (Including a search of
SMERDYAKOV's body.). LUKE goes behind bed and looks
under mattress etc. WALKER comes on.*)

WALKER: What's all the noise? Why has Stepan got that loaf
of bread in his mouth?

LUKE: He's having a fit! I put it there to stop him biting his
tongue.

(*WALKER rushes to take bread out of SMERDYAKOV's mouth and check he's alright.*)

WALKER: He's passed out!

LUKE: He's sleeping. (*Short pause.*) I wish he was dead.

WALKER: Christ, Luke! You must learn to control your anger!

LUKE: How can you control the way you're made? How can you? It's happened.

WALKER: I'm your father. That makes me responsible.

LUKE: A father who screwed up my childhood? Who served up sadness like porridge at breakfast? Maybe!

WALKER: Not quite like that, Luke.

LUKE: You wouldn't know. Did you even know Stepan was ill?

WALKER: I'm sorry. I assumed he was with you. This is why I wanted you to befriend him. Why it was important. In this way I felt he may not dwell on the past and drive himself mad with it. I left him with you to let him…reflect. In safe hands. I've been working on the book.

LUKE: Why might he go mad?

WALKER: (*After a pause.*) The war. You go. I'll watch him. When he wakes I'll tell him you were trying to save his life.

LUKE: Yes, that sounds good. Noble. Powerful. (*Pause. Suddenly breaking down.*) I don't know what to do Dad!

WALKER: What do you mean?

LUKE: She loves him!

WALKER: Who?

LUKE: Natashia.

WALKER: I don't think so.

LUKE: She is in love! Don't tell me about this mysterious person she had the affair with et cetera et cetera I was round at her place this morning and she was sketching his eyes! I know what he's doing. He wants to use his suffering, whatever it is, to seduce her. That's what he's doing. And what can I do against that? You know what she's like, she loves all that stuff. I love her, dad and this bloody…well what is he?…TARTAR!…I know his next move…he's got this cross. Told me the story of how he got it.

WALKER: A cross?

LUKE: I haven't seen it but he's told me the story. He bought it, he says, from someone, he says, who got it from the man who murdered someone to get it. I think he bought it off the murderer! The murderer himself and he knows that it was the murderer but can't admit it because…well, buying the cross off someone who murdered someone else for it would itself be a crime and Stepan would know that because, for all his posing he's not a nihilist and if he was, the cross wouldn't mean anything to him and it does! Now…

WALKER: Slow down, Luke! Too fast!

LUKE: Nearly finished! A cross like that to someone who sings those songs like she does…to a poet…that cross would be the ultimate metaphor, symbol…song. Poem. (*Pause.*)

WALKER: It's an incredible story. I wonder why he told it. He seems to have made it up.

LUKE: Why?

WALKER: Well, because if he did buy it from the murderer, the murderer would have had to admit to it for Stepan to know he'd done it, but would the murderer admit to his crime and risk being shopped by a moralist? You go Luke, I'll get to the bottom of it.

LUKE: Even if the story's made up I know the cross isn't! But I can't find it! I cannot find it! It's a myth! A dream! The delusions of a people besieged by empires! You've got to help me Dad! Tell him to leave off Nat. Please! And if you can get the cross off him…give it to me. PLEASE!

WALKER: If it exists…of course.

(*LUKE leaves.*)

All this illness.

(*WALKER begins to look for the cross. After a moment, SMERDYAKOV wakes.*)

SMERDYAKOV: (*With difficulty.*) George? What are you doing?

WALKER: I have to confess, I'm snooping. I'm looking for the cross.

SMERDYAKOV: Luke told you.

WALKER: Yes. Can I see it?

> (*Silence.*)

> No. Of course. For a moment I almost thought it was here. (*Pause.*) You know that I'm working on a history of what happened out there. I thought I could rely on you to support me in that.

SMERDYAKOV: I do!

WALKER: Then what have you told him about the cross?

SMERDYAKOV: A parable!

WALKER: Parable?

SMERDYAKOV: Yes. That is all.

WALKER: But why? Why anything?

SMERDYAKOV: I do not know. I am stupid.

WALKER: Why are you here?

SMERDYAKOV: Because I need...I need you.

WALKER: O, you mean, my teachings had helped those who prosecuted the war on your side because of my analysis of your history and I was loved; fawned over. And being in the nearness of me conferred reputation...

SMERDYAKOV: No! I need you to save me! I thought you would need me too! We would help each other!

WALKER: Yes! Help each other! But how is this helping? At one point you asked would my soul survive the torment of my own moral judgement. Why did you say that?

SMERDYAKOV: I do not know did I! Did I say that?

WALKER: You know you did, Stepan! What worries me is that you seem ill; unstable – like someone on a mission...to SAVE MY SOUL! But I can deal with my own moral impulses. What I must have is redemption. Isn't it? And you! Redemption! And we can only get that by putting the past behind us!

SMERDYAKOV: Yes!

WALKER: Good, then! Good! That's it!

> (*SMERDYAKOV is tearful.*
> *WALKER cradles SMERYAKOV in his arms.*)

> Stepan. Stepan.

(*WALKER holds SMERDYAKOV tight. He strokes his hair.*
WALKER gently rocks SMERDYAKOV. WALKER leaves.
Lights down.)

Scene Twelve A

Ghosts of GRUSHENKA and SONIA.

SONIA: You don't have to tell me!

GRUSHENKA: I have to! I have to SAY it! I want to know
that it's been SAID: as though written down.

SONIA: Then you'll say it for me too. (*Pause. Uncertainly.*)
What was the first thing?

GRUSHENKA: The men around the fire. All the drunken
soldiery...around that fire...at the end of time...

SONIA: The dance hall...I was nervous...two left feet...the
man touched me...where are you staying tonight? At
home! He was beautiful! The sweet sour smell of wine...he
touched my hand...

GRUSHENKA: No! They were our soldiers! Why did they
turn on us? Because we were the artists?!

SONIA: You are a beautiful woman, he said...

GRUSHENKA: Why weren't they stopped? They took me
– five men. On the banks of a brook...at midnight...

SONIA: He walked me outside...moonlight...took my
hand...said only: I am with you. For ever. Pushed my head
between his legs. Walker. I didn't want it. Smerdyakov
stopped it.

GRUSHENKA: They ripped my clothes off. Every last stitch.
With a man on each limb they pulled me apart... the fifth
came at me with his fist...between my legs... came at me
with his head between my legs; vomited on my lower
body; pissed it off; four men pissed in my mouth buggered
me; ripped out my womb, then the next and the next then
tore me limb from body, limb from body and what was left
they threw into the brook. At midnight.

(*Lights down.*)

Scene Twelve

WALKER and NATASHIA.

WALKER: Natashia, I'm breaking!

NATASHIA: I don't understand!

WALKER: You love him! Stepan!

NATASHIA: George!

WALKER: Before you say anything…I understand: if I look at you, your hair, the way you tie it back – I think of the moment in which you tied it. That purpose. Struggling against the tide of your emotions which are telling you that nothing matters! All is falsehood. The man you loved, devoted yourself to, was a cipher. And you see Stepan and you sink into the palm of that hand that is held out from eternity – the hand of the man who has suffered for what he believes and revealed all our daily trials for the sickeningly petty things they are. I know how Stepan is an object of love and devotion!…

NATASHIA: George! I don't love him! It's you! All that you said then is YOU! I love you!

WALKER: But you can't love me! You can't love me because I can't love you! If I love you then I'm back in the war. No redemption! I am on the trail of tears where all the raped and discarded cower and die.

(NATASHIA holds his face.)

NATASHIA: Be calm! Be calm! I don't understand you. What are you saying?

(She kisses him.)

WALKER: Nothing. It's nothing. O God, Natasha, he is dying! He's dying and there's nothing I can do about it!

(They get onto the sofa.
They kiss as lights go down.)

Scene Thirteen

The same. Night.

Lights come up only a little. NATASHIA and WALKER are asleep on sofa. A sheet covers WALKER, including most of his head.

LUKE comes on.

He tiptoes to the sofa and suddenly puts a hand across NATASHIA's mouth to stop her from speaking etc. She mumbles, shocked.

WALKER stirs and becomes still when he hears LUKE's voice.

LUKE: (*Sotto voce.*) The earrings were a mistake. I feel that more acutely than ever now. Of course I do. Who is this? (*He takes his hand from NATASHIA's mouth.*)

NATASHIA: (*Sotto voce.*) It's the father of my son.
(*NATASHIA gets up carefully from sofa and sits on floor away from sofa.*
LUKE stands near her.)

LUKE: Why are you with him? What if I were to get you something…something you couldn't get anywhere else? No. That's too simple. Let me tell you the story behind this…this thing. This object. Two old men have come to a town for a religious festival. The town is in a war. Everywhere people are dying. Even the church steps are littered with the dead. The two old men have to step over the bodies to get back to their hotel. They weep tears of despair and, perhaps, regret at having failed to leave a better world for their children. Neither drinks. They say their prayers and go righteously to sleep. By the morning one old man has killed the other. Why? Slit his throat. Why? Do you think it may have been the images of death everywhere? The palpable realities of death that they had to pick their way through? Do you think that despair can do this? Well I can get this item, this thing killed for, which contains as much despair as you will ever find in the world. Do you know what it is?

NATASHIA: A tin cross.

LUKE: (*Shocked.*) What? You know?

NATASHIA: The one old man killed the other for a tin cross. But Luke, I'm not interested.
(*Silence.*
LUKE is stunned.)
I've seen it. It means nothing to me.

LUKE: You've seen it?

NATASHIA: Yes.

LUKE: Then it exists! Did you touch it? What did it look like?

NATASHIA: A cross!

LUKE: A cross! Christ! Listen! This thing…in my mind I see temples rising up out of heat and parched hearts. I hear a terrifying music. I see the world resolved in a cheap stone at the crux. I see Samarkand! What did you see?

NATASHIA: I saw a tin cross in a man's hand.

LUKE: Did you hold it?

NATASHIA: No.

LUKE: No?!

NATASHIA: No!

LUKE: You didn't? That cross had been in the hand of a murderer! You didn't hold it? That's not like you!

NATASHIA: What's not like me? How do you know what's not like me? You've made a picture of me. A photograph to sit on your mantelpiece! OK! I DID HOLD IT!

LUKE: You did? What did it feel like?

NATASHIA: Cold.

(*Pause.*
Suddenly LUKE takes NATASHIA by the hair and roughly kisses her.
NATASHIA slaps LUKE.)

LUKE: I'm sorry Natashia! I'm sorry! I'm sorry!

NATASHIA: Get out! Get out!

LUKE: I'm sorry. Pity me.

NATASHIA: Take that man from his cross!

(*NATASHIA gets up.*
LUKE slinks off.
Lights down.)

Scene Fourteen A

Ghost of LEBEDEV.

LEBEDEV: We're slaves to freedom. It's nothing more than a cry of anguish from the dying. We may scourge every principle, deprave every value for this notion of freedom. And what is it? A contentious relativity. We are in the grip of the exploiters of freedom whose strength lies in our fear of denying an idea that seems to possess so much beauty. But freedom is a beauty that isn't there! Just as the sea, great nullifier of time and release from the nausea of temporality, cannot be embraced. For me, freedom exploded with my head.

(*Lights down.*)

Scene Fourteen

LUKE and SMERDYAKOV.

SMERDYAKOV is still in bed.

The four GHOSTS are present.

The women dance a mournful dance and recite the poem.

We hear the faint calling of FRAN, off.

FRAN: Hello!

LUKE: I am empty Stepan. There is only one thing I believe in. The cross. I know now that I cannot live without it. It means so much. Speak to me. Tell me!

SMERDYAKOV: (*Weakly.*) Our group went into a village occupied by our army under General Rogoshin. (*Pause.*) It was known as the village of the women. The men had been forced to kill each other. Or, if they did not kill they were killed by our army. Neighbours, people who had shared growing up; who had attended school and church together, who had played football together, who had played with girls together and learned sex together; who had dreamed of a great world of future together; who had shared the smallest things that bring us the closest together and shared the greatest things – the things that make us excited to be in families with goals beyond horizons. People who had done everything together, were made to do the most terrible things now. To each other. One man would be made to bite off the penis and testicles of another man – his neighbour, knowing that soon someone, another neighbour, would come to bite off his. And they would be left to bleed to death.

(*Pause.*)

LUKE: Come on! Come on!

FRAN: (*Off. Getting a little nearer.*) Hello!

SMERDYAKOV: Some of the men had been away to schools and colleges and the officers making them do these things may have been their teachers. Teachers! People who give us our reason to respect; our reason to believe in whatever: society or authority. Morality! The carnage and the demented men. Death becomes a reward. Later, twenty men took two women into the schoolhouse and there raped them throughout the night. No one slept! Just one incident among many.

LUKE: I told you! And you said: 'Our people don't go to war to rape'!

SMERDYAKOV: Before the rapes we were sitting around a fire. Rogoshin and most of the soldiers were drunk. Our leader was there. Our historian. He was a big man. Handsome! It is true! Out of his eyes seemed to shine goodness – a goodness that had grown, perhaps, a little tired but he looked as if he had a special relationship with life. With the people. And with his mass of hair swept back he looked like a man with great purpose. (*Pause.*) During the agonies of that day and night, one of the villagers said to me: how can a man who looks like this allow these things to happen? But even he had become simply an historical fact.

LUKE: You're talking about my father!

(*SMERDYAKOV begins to speak with difficulty; seems to have difficulty with his breathing etc.*)

FRAN: (*Off, nearer.*) Hello!

SMERDYAKOV: He spoke to the soldiers: 'I have had every woman I have ever made contact with who I wanted to have: any one of my students; any one of my secretaries; even my colleagues secretaries. My WIFE, of course; my wife's SISTER! I like DOING it!' Then he said: 'listen, whatever happens is legitimate. These people must never rise again. History demands this. Read Michelet!' And

Rogoshin said: 'Take the women! You must be sure they will never have children. Take EVERY woman; every woman must be made barren and every barren woman will live to show how we can make deserts of vineyards and put an end to their history. After this village: the next! And the next. Beyond the horizon.'

LUKE: And my father? My father did...

SMERDYAKOV: Nothing. He spoke but did nothing. He gave the idea.

LUKE: What are you saying? He wouldn't have just let it happen!

SMERDYAKOV: He was too flattered by the soldiers to stop them. (*Pause.*) After it was all over, I held up the cross. The prize!

LUKE: The cross!

SMERDYAKOV: One of the Partisans, Alyosha, and one of the leaders Lebedev tried to stop what was happening. I was there when they slit Alyosha's throat. They threw the cross at my feet.

(*SMERDYAKOV lets out an apparently final gasp.*

LUKE is wild with anger. He cries out. He pulls at SMERDYAKOV etc. so that SMERDYAKOV falls out of bed, his head crashing to the floor.

After a moment, WALKER, GRACE and FRAN rush on to find LUKE pulling SMERDYAKOV's bed apart. As LUKE continues, WALKER checks SMERDYAKOV.)

WALKER: He's dead.

(*SMERDYAKOV suddenly sits up.*)

SMERDYAKOV: Lebedev!

GRACE: Who's Lebedev?

WALKER: No one. A traitor.

SMERDYAKOV: Beauty!

(*SMERDYAKOV collapses back onto bed. Dead.*)

WALKER seems to cry. He stands

(*GRACE embraces him.*

FRAN comes to WALKER and looks at his face.)

FRAN: He's not crying! There are no tears! Look into his eyes!

(*GRACE steps back.*)

Look into his eyes! He's PLEASED!

(*THE GHOSTS walk away as GRACE backs off and joins
FRAN from WALKER.*

*WALKER looks at them and shrugs as LUKE continues to tear
the bed apart.*)

WALKER: For Christ's sake, Luke! There is no cross! I
crushed it with my own hand!

End.

the fourth world

characters

helen waldergrave / maria alvarado

charles waldergrave / death squad man

gustavo alvarado escobar

the first scene is set in colombia, all other scenes in the living room of the waldergraves' home:

part one
scene one: colombia. home of maria alvarado. evening.
scene two: britain. home of the waldergraves. evening.
scene three: next day. late afternoon.
scene four: same day. evening.
scene five: next day. morning.
scene six: the lesson. same day. evening.

part two
scene one: late evening.
scene two: next day. early evening.
scene three: later that evening.
scene four: some days later. night.
scene five: later the same night.

set
a room in white.
the predominant shape within the room is the sphere.
there is a lampstand with a large, spherical shade.
there is a bookshelf in a spherical or oval design.
even the furniture should suggest a sphere.
there is a tape recorder also in a spherical or oval design.
in the first scene there is nothing on the bookshelf.
there is a coathanger with nothing on it in part one.
in the second scene, there are no books, only a pile of old newspapers, magazines etc.
they are so neatly stacked, the suggestion is they've never been read.

The first production of *the fourth world* was given by the Made in Wales Stage Company at Theatre Clwyd on 21 February 1990 with the following cast:

helen / maria, Helen Gwynne

charles / death squad man, Nicholas Pritchard

gustavo, Dominic Hingorani

Directed by Gilly Adams

Designed by Kim Kenny

Lighting by Keith Hemming

Stage Management Russell Harvey, Peter Grundy,
Philipa Malbon

thanks to
Toby Robertson, Artistic Director, Theatre Clwyd
Michael Williams, Executive Director, Theatre Clwyd
Cheryl Nance, Casting Director, Theatre Clwyd
Paddy Wilson, Production Manager, Theatre Clwyd
and to all the staff at Theatre Clwyd

thank you to Margaret Rockingham-Gill for the Spanish

part one

scene one

Late evening. Colombia.

The set is bathed in a soft red light with the hint of a blue which troubles it.

MARIA is in nightclothes. She takes a glass of wine from the bookshelf. The first movement of Chopin's piano concerto No 2 in B flat minor is playing. She lays on the sofa and sips the wine listening to the music. All is still for a few moments.

Suddenly, a man dressed in para-military uniform bursts on screaming his words and holding a pistol before him.

MARIA immediately jumps up terrified.

DEATH SQUAD MAN: (*With an unnatural screaming quality.*)
No muevas! ¿Et es tu Maria Alvarado?!
MARIA: (*Terrified.*) ¿C-c-como?
DEATH SQUAD MAN: Tu nombre! ¿Alvarado?
MARIA: Si!
DEATH SQUAD MAN: Gustavo! Necisito a Gustavo?
¿Dónde está?!
MARIA: ¿Gust…?! ¿Gustavo?
(*DEATH SQUAD MAN advances on MARIA. He puts the gun viciously between her legs as if to shoot her in the vagina. MARIA has become speechless with terror. The DEATH SQUAD MAN becomes more and more excited, building to a frenzy hearing the sound of his own voice.*)
DEATH SQUAD MAN: ¿Dónde está? ¿Dónde está Gustavo?!
El niño! Tu hijo? ¿No es tu hijo? ¿Dónde está?!
(*DEATH SQUAD MAN takes MARIA by the hair. MARIA gasps, choking on her terror. DEATH SQUAD MAN brutally pulls her up.*)
Gustavo! Gustavo!

(MARIA can't speak. DEATH SQUAD MAN throws her down behind the sofa.)
(Aiming his gun at her.) Dónde está Gustavo?!
(Silence. He goes down behind sofa. He hits her. MARIA cries out. DEATH SQUAD MAN gets up.)
Esta bien!
(He begins to undo his trousers. He pauses.)
Otra vez. Por la ultima vez! Dónde está Gustavo?
Alvarado!
(MARIA begins crying. DEATH SQUAD MAN goes to undo his trousers again and stops.)
(In American English.) Fuck it!
(He shoots her and goes. After a moment, GUSTAVO appears briefly out of the dark. His face shows incomprehension and horror and incalculable fear. There is a terrible scream but not from him.
Blackout.)

scene two

Early evening. Britain.

The lounge in the Waldergraves' home. There is music playing. It's the last movement of Chopin's Sonata No 2 for Piano.

GUSTAVO is standing alone in the room. He looks lost and perplexed listening to the music. CHARLES comes on carrying a mug of drink.

CHARLES: Gustavo!
   (Silence.)
   (Concerned.) Gustavo? What is it?
   (CHARLES sits.)
   (Teacherly. Enthusiastically.) The music? Are you familiar with it? It's Chopin. It IS perplexing. It's the final movement of his second piano sonata. I call it a coda. Do you understand this? Coda? A section that comes at the end of a larger piece of music. Though it comes out of that piece it seems somehow separate. As though it were beginning something entirely new. In this case it's as if all the forces of his world have sprung apart and he's

68

struggling to put them back together. (*Pause.*) But there's an evil influence preventing the creation of this new world. Like a force of unreason. This is not mere anarchy loosed on the world Gustavo: this is something much more serious because it's developed out of order. (*Pause.*) What is finally perplexing is the last chord.
(*They listen until the end of the piece.*)
Is that triumph or despair? (*Pause.*) You know what I think? I think it's despair but in that despair is triumph. Because it IS a chord. The forces have been put together even if only as a compromise.
(*Silence.*)
What did you want?

GUSTAVO: I have a letter from my parents. They are visiting.

CHARLES: Visiting? From Colombia?

GUSTAVO: Just for the night. They will come for holiday in Great Britain.

CHARLES: Just for a night! Then they'll stay here!

GUSTAVO: No! Not here.

CHARLES: What?

GUSTAVO: It would be problem. They stay in hotel!
(*Pause.*)

CHARLES: (*Caringly.*) Gustavo. I think I understand. (*Pause.*) But wouldn't this be a good opportunity for you to bring some normality back into your life?

GUSTAVO: No, they must not stay here! You DON'T understand.

CHARLES: (*Impatiently.*) Understand what? I'm a teacher! I WANT to understand! So what is it?
(*Silence.*)
(*Reassuringly.*) I know what happened. I have had communication with your father. You know this.

GUSTAVO: I know. And I haven't talked about it with you or Mrs Waldergrave.

CHARLES: Good. It would be upsetting for Helen. (*Pause.*) It would be wonderful for you all as a family to have the night together here. If you like, Gustavo, in the care of the First World!

(*Silence.*)

GUSTAVO: I don't want it.

(*CHARLES gets up. He paces a little angrily.*)

CHARLES: Sometimes it's not enough to be a teacher. Sometimes a teacher needs to be a policeman too.

(*GUSTAVO looks horrified. CHARLES sees this.*)

CHARLES: (*Lightly.*) Don't worry! I'm not going to arrest you! Ha!

(*CHARLES goes to GUSTAVO. He holds him by the shoulders reassuringly.*)

Look, Gustavo. (*Pause.*) What I mean is I have the power to make sure everything is alright. They'll stay.

(*Silence. CHARLES sits again. He senses GUSTAVO's dissatisfaction.*)

(*Suddenly impatient.*) I know why you don't want them to stay. Shall I tell you? I think you've become infatuated with Helen. It's happened before. Appreciation of the beauty of Helen has often been misunderstood by the young men who've stayed.

(*GUSTAVO looks very uncomfortable. He hangs his head a little.*)

You see you're embarrassed! (*Understandingly.*) This is what I'm talking about. What's needed is a policeman! Someone to stop you going the wrong way up a one-way street (*Pause.*) What's happened is, you've created a romantic view of your life here. I know you, you don't want your boring parents et cetera coming in and spoiling the illusion.

(*Silence.*)

I want them to stay because I want them to reassociate you with your past. Because I don't want you having this romantic unrealistic view of life!

GUSTAVO: This is not true. I am just happy here.

CHARLES: Gustavo! You may not see the connections. I do. That's what I meant about teachers and policemen and how they're connected.

GUSTAVO: (*Suddenly losing control.*) Why don't you stop talking about that Charles!

(*GUSTAVO turns to go.*)

CHARLES: Gustavo, you're being absurd! Nevertheless, I put my policeman's hat on and say they stay!
(*Blackout.*)

scene three

Next day.

HELEN is sitting on the floor staring out at the audience. She has her legs folded over each other like a North American Indian, and her arms folded. She is wearing a track suit. There is a glass of wine on the bookcase which she will drink from.

GUSTAVO comes on quietly.

HELEN: Gustavo! Guess what I found out today?
GUSTAVO: I...I don't know.
HELEN: (*Making much of the way she's sitting.*) Guess!
  (*Silence. GUSTAVO shrugs.*)
  Well look at me! What do you think I am?
GUSTAVO: (*Bemused.*) I don't know!
  (*HELEN makes Indian noises by tapping her hand on her mouth.*)
HELEN: Indians! Once I heard that your parents were coming, I went to Smith's. That's a bookshop. I went and I found out that there are Indians in Colombia! (*Pause.*) That's what I am!
  (*GUSTAVO laughs gently.*)
GUSTAVO: Indians yes. But not Hollywood Indians!
  (*HELEN stops.*)
HELEN: What?
GUSTAVO: They are different.
HELEN: Are they?
GUSTAVO: Yes. Well...in a way.
HELEN: In what way?
  (*GUSTAVO sits.*)
GUSTAVO: Well, in North America the Indians were more, you know like fighters. They fought the Americans. But in South America the Spanish conquered the Indian. There was no fight.

HELEN: You make that sound so sad.

(*Silence.*)

You're homesick aren't you?

GUSTAVO: What?

(*Pause.*)

HELEN: I know you.

GUSTAVO: What?

HELEN: There's a deep river running in you. (*Pause.*) You know, there was a time before I met Charles when I was very lonely. That condition is a vulnerable one. People can take advantage of you. (*Pause.*) Why don't you relax?

(*She drinks from her glass of wine.*)

Let me get you some wine.

GUSTAVO: (*As if shocked.*) Wine! No!

HELEN: (*Lightly.*) Good grief Gustavo! You'd have thought I'd given you an electric shock!

GUSTAVO: Wine is not for the young. In our family. It corrupts the innocent.

HELEN: O, well. I don't want to do that! Talking of which – I mean your family – tell me a bit about them. They'll be here next week and I hardly know a thing! What does your father do?

(*GUSTAVO looks glum, perplexed.*)

What's the matter? (*Playfully.*) Don't you like him?

GUSTAVO: Plastics.

HELEN: Sorry?

GUSTAVO: Plastics?

HELEN: Plastics?

GUSTAVO: Yes! Plastics! (*With a hint of bitterness.*) He makes plastics. His factory is Plastios Melin L…T… D…A… And HIS father… (*Pause. A little calmer.*) My grandfather he also owns a plastic factory called Gilpa. HIS plastics they use in the supermarkets like Carulla, Ley and Cafam. And in my father's he makes… (*Points to lampshade.*) This.

HELEN: That? Lampshades?

GUSTAVO: Yes. This kind of thing. Beautiful in plastics!

HELEN: And what about you? What do you want to do? Do you want to make plastics?

GUSTAVO: (*Very seriously.*) No! I want to be a vet.

HELEN: (*Sympathetically.*) O, Gustavo! (*Pause. She half gets up.*) That's it isn't it!? That's why you're so sad! I've discovered the real you! I understand your tragedy: you want to be a vet and your father wants you to make plastic bags. (*Pause.*) What's his name?

GUSTAVO: Nestor. Nestor Escobar.

HELEN: Peculiar name. And your mother?

GUSTAVO: (*After a pause.*) Juanita.

HELEN: Juanita! I like that! That sounds like cha, cha, cha! That's the kind of time we'll have when they're here! A JuanITA cha, cha, cha time! Don't worry, I'll make sure everything goes well. I'll put them at ease. (*Pause.*) Even if it means I have to read a history of Colombia from the year dot!
(*She laughs and puts a hand on GUSTAVO's leg.*)
I'll take care of you!
(*GUSTAVO seems a little uncomfortable.*)

GUSTAVO: Where...where is Charles?
(*HELEN takes her hand away.*)

HELEN: At a political meeting. He's what he calls a radical. (*Pause.*) Do you know anything about politics?

GUSTAVO: It is like wine. Forbidden the young.
(*Pause.*)

HELEN: (*Suspecting something.*) Charles hasn't said anything to you has he?

GUSTAVO: Said?

HELEN: (*Angrily.*) Charles thinks I'm...stupid! He thinks I'm not mature enough to discuss the things I talk about. It's just middle-class shit!
(*She suddenly stops and puts a hand to her mouth. Silence. GUSTAVO hides his surprise.*)
(*With mock shame. Playfully.*) Sorry, I...

GUSTAVO: I like it here... I just don't want Charles to think I'm trying to... (*He makes a snake-like gesture.*) ...with your family.

HELEN: I don't know... (*Pause.*) Worm?

GUSTAVO: Worm?

HELEN: You know...worm...

(They suddenly see the humour in this. HELEN makes an exaggerated almost sexual gesture of worming.)
Worm your way into the family.
GUSTAVO: *(Laughing.)* Yes. It sounds funny!
(Pause.)
HELEN: Why would you worm your way in?
(Pause. Laughter.)
GUSTAVO: Why? I don't know!
(They laugh.)
HELEN: *(Enjoying this.)* No, I mean when people worm their way in it's to...you know...SNEAK their way in as if it's to get in without being noticed. I'm sure people say I wormed my way into the middle-class by marrying Charles! They say WORMED when they mean someone's doing something for a different reason from the one they'd have if they just came straight in! *(Pause.)* We had a French boy staying once. A French JEWish boy. Charles sent him home. Charles now says that it's because he wanted to protect me from the holocaust! That wasn't the reason the boy was sad. He was sad because he was homesick and that's why he went home! See?
GUSTAVO: *(Worriedly.)* Holo...holo... What is this holo...cist?
HELEN: Holocaust. Nothing. Don't worry yourself.
GUSTAVO: But I am worried about...about *(Uncertainly.)* romantic things? What does it mean?
(HELEN looks intrigued.)
HELEN: Love?
GUSTAVO: O, no. I don't think love.
HELEN: You're not talking, are you, about sex?
GUSTAVO: Is it? I am sorry, this is wrong.
HELEN: Not necessarily!
GUSTAVO: Then it is the same.
HELEN: What?
GUSTAVO: Well...for example, in our country, they try to stop us reading the books of Gabriel Garcia Marquez...
HELEN: *(Interestedly.)* I've never heard of him.
GUSTAVO: Some say he has turned the country into...um ...bordello. You know? This house of sex.

HELEN: Sounds revolting!

GUSTAVO: Yes! You mean like in revolution. This is what is not liked.

HELEN: (*Laughs.*) Actually, I meant something else. Never mind. Either way it's probably true.

GUSTAVO: There is a place called Macondo in the books. This is the Colombia of Marquez. It is a place of evil...we are told. Colombia is very religious. So we are told this writer is blasphemous. But the boys and the young men have the books. We have read...I have read...

HELEN: (*Mischievously.*) The naughty bits?

GUSTAVO: (*Embarrassed.*) Well... But it causes trouble. This is what I mean.

HELEN: You mean you're worried about reading the book?

GUSTAVO: No. I am worried because sex stops us reading the book. And perhaps the book can help us learn.

HELEN: So in other words, it's got nothing to do with the sex they just don't want you to read the book!

GUSTAVO: Yes. You understand. You are very intelligent. (*Pause.*)

HELEN: Why don't you do something for him? For your father? To show him how well you're getting on with your work learning English.

GUSTAVO: Don't I speak well?

HELEN: O, yes. But you want to show him that YOU understand. That's different.

(*HELEN puts a hand on GUSTAVO's knee again. As if she's had a revelation.*)

Why don't you make something in plastic? Show your understanding in plastic! You need to raise yourself in the eyes of your father. You need to show your father that you're far less stupid than he thinks you are. Then he might let you be a vet and all your troubles will be over! I'm sure Charles will help.

GUSTAVO: I don't know. Anyway, what could I make for HIM. Especially in plastic! (*Pause.*) I will tell you about him. Many fathers in Colombia are like this. They hate their sons. Because the son is young and growing handsome.

HELEN: I don't believe that! They wouldn't send you all the way over if they didn't love you!

GUSTAVO: But you can see it! The father dresses like a cowboy. He has moustaches and oil on his hair to be young! They ride around on their horses with six guns.

HELEN: What matters is that you give him something only you can give him.

(*CHARLES comes on. He stands for a moment looking in silence at GUSTAVO and HELEN. He looks perplexed. HELEN gets up when she sees him.*)

Hiya Charlie!

(*She goes to him and gives him a hug and a kiss.*)

We've just been discussing Gustavo's parents' visit. Juanita and (*To GUSTAVO*) what was it?

CHARLES: Nestor.

HELEN: Gustavo's going to need a bit of help with them. Especially with his father.

(*CHARLES takes his coat off. GUSTAVO gets up to go.*)

The father's the hunter, the son is the sensitive poet.

GUSTAVO: I will go to bed.

(*HELEN seems annoyed with things.*)

HELEN: Sensitive and intelligent

CHARLES: Night!

(*GUSTAVO goes. CHARLES sits.*)

HELEN: (*A little angrily.*) I don't understand. You arrive, he goes. This is ridiculous.

CHARLES: (*Gently.*) Helen, you're awfully naive. He's a young man. How do you know what a young man like that feels?

HELEN: The world is YOUR oyster, but it's not mine. I only make contact with it when we have your students staying. What's wrong with that?

CHARLES: Nothing's wrong with it, it's just not… ultimately…the way we live.

HELEN: What do you mean?

CHARLES: Getting involved. It's not the function of our culture. Not part of our curriculum! We teach. But we don't get involved with those we teach.

HELEN: I think you're making a mountain out of a molehill! (*Pause.*) Gustavo wants to be a vet. Did you know that? And they won't let him. They want to turn a sad, sensitive boy into a fat greedy man. That's the way I see it.

CHARLES: (*Incredulously.*) What!

HELEN: Well he IS sad. Wouldn't you say?
(*CHARLES sighs dismissively.*)
They want to make him spend his life making plastic! His father owns a plastic factory.

CHARLES: I know.

HELEN: You know! Well I didn't! (*Gasps frustratedly.*) I had a wonderful idea. That Gustavo could make something for his father, out of plastic, that would show his father how well he's doing here! (*Short pause.*) Want to help?
(*Silence.*)
You know, Charlie, there's something very cold about you sometimes. I can understand how important this whole business is to Gustavo. I can understand it because I can sympathise. The trouble with people like you is you know too much for anyone else's good. But people like me and Gustavo don't and that makes us vulnerable. We need help!
(*Silence. CHARLES draws HELEN to him. Pause. He kisses her.*
Blackout.)

scene four

There is a large, South American Indian blanket on the back of the sofa.

CHARLES is sitting on the sofa. He's looking off expectantly. He is reading a tabloid newspaper.

HELEN comes on. She has a towel around her shoulders as if she's been exercising. She stops suddenly.

HELEN: (*About blanket.*) What's this?

CHARLES: It's an Indian blanket. We want the Escobars to feel at home.

HELEN: (*About the tabloid paper.*) Why are you reading that? Isn't it more a paper for the likes of me?

(*HELEN goes to the pile of papers. She begins to take papers from the pile one by one. She places them on the floor and looks carefully into each one.*)

CHARLES: I've never said that! Stop putting yourself down!

HELEN: I can see you saying it! Maybe not about me but about the kind of people I come from.

CHARLES: O right, we're back there. Actually, I confiscated it from Gustavo.

(*HELEN turns to him angrily.*)

HELEN: Why did you do that?!

CHARLES: (*Surprised.*) What?

(*HELEN gets up. She snatches the paper from CHARLES.*)

HELEN: You confiscate something from somebody and you hurt them! It's an act of violence!

(*She throws the paper on his lap.*)

CHARLES: I tell you I couldn't look his father in the eye knowing that his son has become clouded with pessimism.

HELEN: What pessimism? What are you talking about?

CHARLES: What this does (*Waving paper*) is it gives you just enough information to make you depressed about the world you live in but not enough to encourage you to think that there's anything you can do about it.

HELEN: Well how is he supposed to understand you confiscating something he could have bought from a shop on the corner? I hope you didn't upset him. It IS only a comic.

(*HELEN goes back to looking through papers.*)

CHARLES: I'm sure he's tougher than you think. Anyway, you're wrong. A comic is a work of childhood literature. It has completeness. (*Indicates paper.*) That is a reduction of the word to a level where it insults even the simplest kid.

HELEN: Don't bully him. Someone's shown him something that's funny and maybe attractive to him. And it IS part of our curriculum.

CHARLES: You can't have correct choice until you know right from wrong.

HELEN: O, no. This isn't really a question of what's right and wrong. Is it? It's a question of what's the right paper. If it was wrong but in the right paper it'd be right.

CHARLES: I didn't confiscate the paper. I borrowed it.

HELEN: Well why didn't you say that?

CHARLES: Because I'm trying to show you that Gustavo is like any other boy. I WOULD normally confiscate a paper like this.

(HELEN returns to papers. She spreads paper on floor.)

HELEN: Do you think if I look through these intellectual papers that it'll give me something to talk to Gustavo's parents about? Something about Colombia?

CHARLES: I think you might discover that the world is not as plastic as you imagine. *(Pause.)* It's not as susceptible to your desire to mould it as you think. *(Pause. Playfully.)* While we're on this: if the idea is that you create this thing to somehow reflect Gustavo's spell at summer school, there are a few things you might consider. Like country of origin of child. Naturally. Wealth of parents; the extent to which parent is buying a holiday for son to get him out of the way or, conversely, the extent to which parent actually WANTS son educated. That country of origin is in Third World where prospects for the well-educated are good. Then there is the determination and commitment of the teacher, not to mention the school; the environment and the general curriculum of the country the child finds itself in. Whether the child likes our cooking or not; whether he can swim and whether we take him swimming or to the zoo. Then, the predilections of the father, what the father might see from his ethical position as the most important manifestation of a month's education in the use of English; whether the father has any use of it himself; what's the father's inner vision – in relationship to his son; what the father's relationship might BE with the son and what he might want his son to become. (*Pause.*) What he was thinking about on the plane over, whether they were held up at customs; whether he blames or adores his wife for giving them Gustavo. (*Caringly.*) Do you think, Helen, that it's possible to put all that into something plastic?

HELEN: I've found something!

(*Silence.*)

Charlie! I've found something!

CHARLES: What?

HELEN: There's a report here from Colombia.

(*CHARLES peers over at the paper.*)

CHARLES: (*Dismissively.*) It's two years old!

HELEN: Listen. It's about the killing of someone called Jaime Pardo Leal who was leader of the Union Patriotic – ah – the Patriotic Union. I'll read what it says 'Bogota' (*Aggressively.*) I found the piece ONLY because I now know that Bogota is the capital of Colombia! Anyway 'The Colombian Minister of Justice, issued an official communique following the assassination of Jaime Pardo Leal blah, blah, blah, stating that so far all investigations have shown that the killing had no political motivation' and 'was undoubtedly linked to drug trafficking'. (*Pause.*) That's it.

(*Pause. He takes the paper and reads.*)

CHARLES: Why would they do it? Why would drug traffickers kill a politician? Unless it was an accident.

(*He throws the paper back at her.*)

HELEN: Accident? How could it be an accident if they killed him?

CHARLES: In the sense that perhaps he was caught in the crossfire between rival gangs. It says that the killing was undoubtedly linked to drug trafficking. What does that mean? That the politician was a drug trafficker? It's more likely that the Minister of Justice is.

HELEN: Why?

CHARLES: Well if the Justice Minister is NOT getting shot by drug traffickers and an opposition politician IS, then

it's quite likely that the Justice Minister is in cahoots with
the drug traffickers. I think this is a political assassination
and the drug traffickers are blamed to make it look like
something else. (*Pause.*) The Minister of Justice puts
on his drug-trafficker's hat to kill the politician. It's a
bit Shakespearean but there it is. Latin America. The
fact that it got so little coverage then suggests that it's
commonplace.

HELEN: Commonplace? In Colombia?

CHARLES: (*Lightly.*) O, no, leave it Helen.

HELEN: For me Charles, if it's commonplace it means it's on
the streets and might explain why Gustavo wants to be a
vet.

CHARLES: OK. Supposing you discover that Colombia is
obsessed with political assassination? Is that what you want
to talk about with his parents? Or do you think you can put
that into your piece of plastic?

HELEN: But aren't you interested in finding out more?
Where's your teacher's inquisitive instinct? (*Pause.*) You do
have one don't you?

CHARLES: No.

HELEN: What?

CHARLES: About this no!

HELEN: Why?

CHARLES: Because I'm not going to teach it!

HELEN: What do you mean?

CHARLES: I'm not interested.

HELEN: How can you say that Charlie? You're a geography
teacher! You're teaching a Colombian student and you're
not interested in his country?

CHARLES: That's exactly right.

HELEN: What?

CHARLES: (*Getting up.*) We don't teach politics in our
schools. It's not part of the curriculum. It's as simple as
that.

HELEN: Why not?

CHARLES: (*Gently.*) I don't know. I suppose because we
don't need to. (*He kisses her.*) I'm whacked! Why don't you,

tomorrow, look through my books? I'm sure you'll find what you need to know. And tonight…well, dream of the blue Caribbean washing the shores of the Uraba region and Gustavo's farm with its green fields slipping gently to the sea. Night love. (*He begins to go.*)

HELEN: You know, you say you're not interested in Colombia but you've bought that Indian blanket as though you are. THAT's interesting!
(*Blackout.*)

scene five

Next day. Morning.

HELEN hurries into room followed by CHARLES. They are trying hard not to shout but occasionally find it impossible not to.

HELEN is very angry. CHARLES is waving a rolled-up broadsheet newspaper.

CHARLES: I'm trying very hard to be patient and reasonable…

HELEN: You had no right!

CHARLES: But now you're stepping over the line! Whatever you found out…

HELEN: You've got no right to put me down in front of Gustavo!

CHARLES: He's my responsibility!

HELEN: Why is he your responsibility? Don't I live here?

CHARLES: (*Calmly.*) Listen. He's here as a student. TO LEARN ENGLISH! That's all. If you want to find out about Colombia why don't you ask me!

HELEN: (*With incredulity.*) What?

CHARLES: (*Very angry.*) I teach Geography! What do you want to know about Colombia? Colombia: It lies between the latitudes of 4C South and 12C North. Its one thousand miles of coast to the North are washed by the waters of the Caribbean while its eight hundred miles of coast to the West by the Pacific. The area is four hundred and thirty-nine odd thousand square miles which includes the

Archipelago de San Andres y Providencia, located in the
Caribbean off the coast of Nicaragua and the islands of
Rosario and San Bemardo in the Caribbean and Gorgona
and Malepo in the Pacific. It's bounded by the countries of
Ecuador, Peru, Brazil, Venezuela and Panama. Part of its
boundary with Venezuela is formed by the Rio Orinoco.
Other rivers include the Rio Guaviare, the Rio Meta,
the Rio Cauca, the Rio Caqueta and the Rio Magdalena.
Demographically, about a third of its population lives in
cities of over 100,000 inhabitants, the capital being Bogota,
a city of some two and a half million. In 1963 – the most
recent year for which I have figures – about a third of
its population was middle-class and about a third were
engaged in agriculture. Its two main political parties are
the Conservatives and the Liberals – the two parties which
have shared power since the country's independence.
Finally, its two main exports in 1975, again the most recent
year for which I have figures, as in 1955, were coffee and
oil though there is a big banana industry in the Uraba
region on the Caribbean Coast.
(HELEN shakes her head with incredulity.)
HELEN: *(Ironically.)* Very clever but what about the plastics?
Your Geography is history.
CHARLES: Helen! You're just not listening to me!
HELEN: I don't think that we can live in this world knowing
that there are people in some kind of pain and not do
something about it. Especially when they're in our home!
(Pause.)
CHARLES: Very well! Let's suppose you're right. But you
said that his problem was to do with him wanting to be a
vet and that that desire was at odds with what his father
wants for him.
HELEN: Yes.
CHARLES: Well what has that got to do with what you found
out about what's happening in Medellin?
HELEN: Gustavo's family's in Medellin! That's where he's
from!
CHARLES: I know, I know. Please don't be obtuse! I'm really
trying to help in this. The whole WORLD knows about

Medellin and its drug problem, and I'm sure Gustavo
and his father have discussed it like any other reasonable
family. But what's the connection between Gustavo's small
worry and a global issue like the Medellin drug cartel!
(*Pause. HELEN looks at CHARLES with incredulity. She
snatches the paper from him.*)

HELEN: The report wasn't about drugs! You never even gave
me chance to read from it!
(*She opens the paper and reads from it. GUSTAVO looks on.*)
'Amnesty International in a report following the
assassination of left-wing opposition leader Jamie Pardo
Leal, says that the claim of the Colombian Minister
of Justice that Dr Pardo was killed by drugs traffickers
is nonsense. Dr Pardo's death followed the killings in
MEDELLIN of leaders of a march which was in response
to a wave of political killings which had claimed the lives
of five students and four lecturers (*Pause.*) at the University
of Antioquia...'

CHARLES: Put things in perspective: Nixon killed as many at
Kent University in the States. It happens.

HELEN: 'Four of the leaders who had led the march were
gunned down within two weeks of its taking place.'

CHARLES: Keep perspective! Thirteen were gunned down in
Derry AS it took place!

HELEN: (*Impatiently.*) 'The wave of killings in Medellin,
coincided with the appearance throughout the country
of "hit lists" in the name of so-called "death squads". In
October, the death squads claimed the life of Dr Pardo for
opposing, courageously, their activities.' Medellin is where
Gustavo lives! (*Pause.*) He MUST know something about
it! You said yesterday that partial knowledge can leave you
pessimistic. Depressed. No future. That's what you said.
Well maybe Gustavo knows something about all this but
not enough!

CHARLES: Ah! So now you DON'T believe his problem is
the vet business?

HELEN: I don't know. I just don't know!

CHARLES: (*Angrily.*) That's right! You don't know!

(*GUSTAVO looks disturbed as if he's on the verge of saying something but holding back. GUSTAVO goes.*)

It's not wise, not even proper to involve yourself with the workings of a strange culture, curriculum, ethos whatever you want to call it! You can know it, respect it, glorify it, envy it, be astounded by it, even use it! But if you interfere you do damage. You'll damage Gustavo.

HELEN: What's damaging Gustavo is not being taught enough!

CHARLES: You don't teach everything. Let me draw you a picture: Supposing I told my geography pupils – that our system of government was, IS corrupt. I could say, for example: it's been using public money to advertise the selling off of public assets on the cheap. Then members of the government buy shares in those public sell-offs and make a killing when the shares are floated and the real value – a high value encouraged by the slick advertising – is realised. I'd make a plausible argument that our government is corruptly using its public power to make private money.

HELEN: Is that true?!

CHARLES: Yes, BUT…

HELEN: You haven't told me this before!

CHARLES: Because…

HELEN: Teach me Charles! Why marry a teacher if you don't get taught?

CHARLES: The government makes the laws and it IS legal. This government belongs to the same consensus, political curriculum that we belong to. The same as the one we all in the Western World belong to. It's called liberal democracy. The feeling is that if a teacher taught what I just said within that curriculum THAT teacher would be irresponsible. Just think about this: if my liberalism causes me to claim that the democracy I believe in is undemocratic, then the liberalism I'm espousing is illiberal because liberalism is synonymous with democracy!

HELEN: (*Surprised.*) O! To tell the truth is illiberal? That's a shock. Well if these reports are the truth then your liberal papers are illiberal. And while we're on this, it's not very liberal to put me down in front of Gustavo!

CHARLES: I'm sorry about that but sometimes...

HELEN: Go on! Blame me! As far as I'm concerned, as a teacher you've got a duty to teach. To open up the world to children and young people.

CHARLES: Only within the parameters of the curriculum!

HELEN: That's shit Charlie! Don't you think you have an obligation to tell your children what you know about the world?

CHARLES: No.

HELEN: Not as a geographer?

CHARLES: No.

HELEN: Nor as a liberal?

CHARLES: No, I've explained that.

HELEN: Well explain this, because I'm stupid: if a liberal is a free-thinker, how can a teacher be a liberal if he's locking away information that'll help children to think freely? (*Silence.*)

CHARLES: The teacher makes decisions within...

HELEN: (*Scornfully.*) The curriculum!

CHARLES: (*Angrily.*) Yes! All we've got is the nation's curriculum! Without it there's anarchy. We don't show pornography to children in order to teach them about SEX.

HELEN: Why not?

CHARLES: (*Surprised.*) Why not?

HELEN: Yes!

CHARLES: Because we need to protect them from pornography!

HELEN: Well maybe you could protect them better if they knew a little more about sex!

CHARLES: That's a bit like saying you can protect children from fascism by teaching them to be illiberal. It doesn't work.

HELEN: I'm not surprised. Liberals aren't allowed to teach the truth!

CHARLES: We're talking about Gustavo! The fact is,
   Gustavo's country is VERY religious and they're
   very sensitive about the sex issue. (*Pause.*) Would you,
   freethinker, take responsibility for teaching him about sex
   when they won't?
   (*Pause.*)
HELEN: (*Angrily.*) Gustavo is hardly a child! Anyway, I think
   as a liberal you ought to teach ANYthing. The only way
   out of this for you as a liberal teacher is to learn as little as
   possible then you won't betray your liberalness by holding
   things back. I don't know why you bother to read the
   Guardian at all. You teachers may as well all read *The Sun.*
   That way, you won't learn more than you're allowed to
   teach!
   (*She throws the paper at him. She begins to go.*)
   And in order to teach Geography, you shouldn't learn
   about the world!
CHARLES: Currently I'm not teaching Geography. I'm
   teaching English to foreign students. And as a teacher of
   English I'm not obliged to teach anything about Colombia!
   (*Silence.*)
   Ultimately, the system – the curriculum, takes
   responsibility for what I don't know.
HELEN: (*Angrily.*) And what you won't admit to knowing!
   (*HELEN looks at him with disgust.*)
   Maybe if I write to Amnesty International they'll tell me
   what I want to know.
   (*Blackout.*)

scene six
the lesson

Same day. Evening.

On the bookshelf is the book Ulysses *by James Joyce. HELEN comes on
with two large glasses of red wine. She puts the glasses on the bookshelf.
She picks up the book and looks towards the end where there is a piece
of paper inserted. She reads and shrugs. She closes the book and puts it*

back on the shelf. She places the book so that the indicating paper can be seen.

Silence.

GUSTAVO comes on.

HELEN: I've brought you some wine.
(She takes the glasses. She gives one to GUSTAVO.)
No getting out of it! *(Pause.)* I know they won't let you drink at home. They don't want you to grow up. I think that a drink at your age is actually good for your health. For your mental health.
(She points to her head. She laughs. She hands wine to GUSTAVO.)
GUSTAVO: I must know…is Charles still not home because you had this row with him this morning about me?
HELEN: What did you hear?
GUSTAVO: Only noise…as I passed through the kitchen.
HELEN: *(Kindly.)* Sit down. Charles is out. Doing his duty. With his political friends. They've got a dinner. Which is why I cooked for you. For us, a row is like a six mile hike. It keeps our minds fit. You worry too much my little Colombian. Sit down. Take a deep breath and let your back sink into that chair.
(GUSTAVO drinks. HELEN lays on the sofa, on her side, facing GUSTAVO.)
I saw a play once. A man was trying to seduce a woman by reciting to her a menu he'd remembered from the days when he was young and a great lover!
(GUSTAVO shrugs.)
GUSTAVO: I don't understand.
HELEN: What is it you don't understand, my brave? Seduce?
GUSTAVO: Yes.
HELEN: How can I explain it? *(Pause.)* When a man – or a woman – wants a woman or a man to let him or her enter her or his…mind. *(Pause.)* For the purpose of making love.
(Silence.)
In the play, the man had compared eating with having sex and an expert lover with a gastronome – someone who

knows a lot about cooking and eating. And he said that a man who treats eating as an animal function, would leave his diners with no experience of the profound love they should have for food, just as in sex, he would leave his mistress with a belly ache! (*She laughs.*) Do you see what he was doing?

GUSTAVO: You mean the menu?

HELEN: In the play, what he was doing was making a metaphor of the menu. A metaphor...do you know what I mean? Metaphor? (*Pause.*) I don't suppose Charles would have got onto that yet. Think of a picture. A picture of one thing to describe another. Like a tree. When they talk about tree of life. Do you understand?

GUSTAVO: Yes.

HELEN: His menu was a metaphor for the act of love he could no longer do. In a way, the recitation of the menu becomes the love-making. It shows that sex is something to be enjoyed in the way that you enjoy a meal and not something to be scared about. Not something you must grow up and feel guilty about. (*Pause.*) Do you know what I mean?

GUSTAVO: Yes! (*Pause.*) Of course.

HELEN: Because you read it in your book by the man who's prohibited?

GUSTAVO: Marquez?

HELEN: Yes.

GUSTAVO: Yes.

HELEN: With friends in some secret place?

GUSTAVO: What do you mean?

HELEN: (*With a little laugh.*) Not what YOU think! It doesn't matter. Shall we play a game?

GUSTAVO: (*Eagerly.*) What game?

HELEN: Strip Jack Naked.

GUSTAVO: (*Shocked.*) What? Naked!... This is?...

HELEN: (*Laughing.*) Joking! (*Pause.*) No, a game like chess. You know how to play chess?

GUSTAVO: (*Enthusiastically.*) Yes!

HELEN: OK. Only there's no board.

GUSTAVO: But how?...

HELEN: And you're after my queen and I'm after your king. And instead of putting each other in check, the object of the game is to seduce each other. I mean, of course, in the game. So the one who wins has seduced the other. OK? After that...after the game, I want you to read something for me. No I should say, if you win.

GUSTAVO: Good!

HELEN: You like reading?

GUSTAVO: I like reading very much.

HELEN: But if I win, I read.

GUSTAVO: Not so good!

(*He laughs.*)

HELEN: How can we play chess without a board?

GUSTAVO: I don't know!

HELEN: It's another metaphor! The chess board is just a picture to show us what's going on. (*She points to her head.*) In there. It's a picture of an argument. The purpose of the game is to put each other's king in check. Yes?

GUSTAVO: Yes!

HELEN: So if the players were to speak they'd say: I want to put your king in check. D'you see that?

GUSTAVO: Yes!

HELEN: So can you think of a similar line to start us off?

GUSTAVO: (*After some thought.*) No!

(*They laugh.*)

HELEN: Well what about this. What if you begin by saying: I want to seduce your queen?

GUSTAVO: OK.

(*Pause.*)

HELEN: Go on then!

(*Pause.*)

GUSTAVO: (*Hesitantly.*) I want to put your queen in...

HELEN: No, Gustavo! I want to SEDUCE your queen!

GUSTAVO: Ah, yes. I want to seduce your queen.

HELEN: OK. Now it would be my turn. I say something or make a direct move. If for example I ask a question and you give me the right answer, you move closer to putting me in check. In other words, seducing me. OK?

(*Pause.*)

OK? You understand that?

GUSTAVO: Yes!

HELEN: Good. Now, in chess, if they used words, the attacker
would declare he's going to check his opponent. So
wouldn't the defender say: to defend myself I'm going to
set out to put YOU in check?

GUSTAVO: Yes.

HELEN: Good. So in our game, once you've declared your
intention to seduce me, what do you think my reaction
would be? What would I say?

(*Pause.*)

GUSTAVO: To defend myself, you must let me seduce...

(*Pause.*)

HELEN: Yes, go on.

GUSTAVO: You must let me seduce you.

HELEN: Yes. Yes, that's good! Because if we're going to play
this game of seduction, you can only set out to seduce your
opponent if you accept that your opponent is quite capable
of seducing you! If we're equals. And that's how it should
be in life. You see? You've moved closer to winning; to
seducing me already. But only because I'm letting you and
because you accept that. Now it's your move.

GUSTAVO: Should I ask a question?

HELEN: You can. Or you can make a direct move.

(*Pause.*)

GUSTAVO: What if I say I want to seduce you because I love
you?

(*Pause.*)

HELEN: OK. (*Pause.*) The only way I can stop you winning
this move is to ask you a question that you can't answer or
give you an answer to the question you've asked! (*Pause.*)
You want to seduce me because you want to MAKE LOVE
TO ME. That's what it means. Which means you're not
being sincere and can't POSSIBLY love me!

GUSTAVO: Why?

HELEN: Because a man's love for a woman is different from
his desire which is what you're talking about when you talk
about making love. His LOVE is selfless but his desire is

SELFISH. So to want to make love to me is not to want to
love me. So you're not being sincere.

GUSTAVO: O, but that is easy to win. I just say I don't know
how to make love.

(*Pause.*)

HELEN: I think you've won that one too. You're moving
closer to winning!

(*GUSTAVO smiles broadly.*)

Now it's my move again. (*Pause.*) Love has been declared.
The first move is made and established. Now we have the
first direct move.

(*Silence.*)

I look for a long time at your mouth which I've watched
with its trembling and I look into your eyes with their other
worlds and I let myself succumb and I KISS you.

(*Pause.*)

GUSTAVO: I won again!

HELEN: What?

GUSTAVO: You have shown me! So I win the move because
you are in defence showing me how to attack! It is simple.
Ha! Ha!

HELEN: Hmmm. That's clever. I suppose you're right!

(*Pause.*) Your move!

(*Pause.*)

GUSTAVO: I don't know.

HELEN: What?!

GUSTAVO: I don't know next move. What to do. What to
say!

(*Pause.*)

HELEN: You win! You win that move.

GUSTAVO: What?

HELEN: Don't act the innocent with me!

GUSTAVO: But I am not acting! It is the truth!

(*HELEN laughs.*)

HELEN: That's how you won it.

GUSTAVO: I don't understand.

HELEN: You've shown naivety; INNOCENCE. Even
vulnerability. And not to win the game. But GENUINELY.

It's part of your character and so I'm not under threat. And
you're learning from the game.

GUSTAVO: Yes?

HELEN: When you learn maths, it's not just to do sums as
exercises. It's to deal with problems in life.

GUSTAVO: I don't understand.

HELEN: It doesn't matter. You're learning that in a
relationship with a woman, the man should show
weakness. It's the woman who should be strong because
she is not aggressive. (*Pause.*) MY move!
(*Pause.*)
I must put my hand...on you. I must put my hand beneath
your shirt to feel your skin.
(*Silence.*)
I think I've won that one. (*Pause.*)

GUSTAVO: (*Sheepishly.*) Unless...unless I take your hand
and...and help you!
(*Silence. HELEN is wide-eyed. She picks up the* Ulysses.)

HELEN: I think you've won. (*Pause.*) We'll do a deal.
Tomorrow I want you to go to a big book shop in town
– Smiths or somewhere and buy your Colombian book for
me and in return you can take this.
(*She hands him the book opening it where the paper is.*)

GUSTAVO: OK!

HELEN: I was showed bits of this when I was in college.
(*Pause.*) Read what I've underlined.
(*GUSTAVO takes the book. Sound of a door banging.*)
O, God, no! There's Charles! Hide the book! Take it and
read where I've got the paper.
(*GUSTAVO hides the book.*)
(*HELEN fusses as if she needs to make things look normal. They
look guiltily at CHARLES as he comes on.*)
Hiya Charlie! I was just giving Gustavo a lesson.

GUSTAVO: I am going to bed. Goodnight.

HELEN: Goodnight Gustavo.

CHARLES: Goodnight Gustavo.
(*GUSTAVO goes.*)
A lesson in what?

HELEN: What?

CHARLES: Come on Helen.

HELEN: (*Without thinking.*) Politics.

(*CHARLES is dumbfounded.*)

CHARLES: (*Angrily.*) I told you! YOU gave him a lesson! OK.
I'll tell you…I'll give YOU a political lesson.

(*CHARLES waves a document.*)

This Amnesty report will tell you why Colombia is
different; why they belong in the Third World. Because
they are obsessed with death, dying, killing, murder, call it
whatever you like.

(*HELEN looks perplexed, almost tearful.*)

This morning you wanted to ask Gustavo whether he
noticed anything unusual in Medellin. And you say you do
this to help him. Whose criteria are you using?

HELEN: I'm sorry Charlie. Let's leave it.

(*HELEN breaks away from CHARLES and sits on the sofa
with her head in her hands. CHARLES speaks from behind
the sofa.*)

CHARLES: In the heart of the holocaust it was not unusual
for Jewish men to get up from the place where they waited
in the room where they waited with women and children
and hang themselves rather than be gassed. It wasn't
unusual! Nobody stirred. If you asked them did anything
unusual happen, you could cause a mass psychosis. So how
can you ask Gustavo whether he noticed anything unusual
happening in Medellin? In OUR cities, in the great cities of
the First World, old people are mugged, women are raped,
women are gang-raped by young men on the piss – out
for a night. Children are murdered, assaulted, abused,
beaten up, tortured. In Northern Ireland, death squads
kill almost at random. If you ask whether there's anything
unusual you may cause a mass psychosis! In Poland, the
wily Polish peasant summed up the carnage that took
place at the bottom of his garden as the trains unloaded
the unsuspecting Jews onto the ramps to be undressed and
deflead, in this simple cold-blooded gesture. (*He draws his
finger across his throat.*) If you go to Poland and ask whether

anything unusual happened, outside the parameters of the ethos which has come to terms with certain events, you could cause a mass psychosis! Children have a view of the world which is a safe view. They trust the world to be there as it was yesterday, on every new day. If you drop bombs on them they become shell-shocked, disorientated, fearful, reactionary: you create a mass psychosis! If you ask Gustavo whether anything unusual happened in Medellin, you may be dropping bombs on him. If you put Gustavo's parents at my table and ask them about the unusual happenings in Medellin or if you continue to give lessons to Gustavo on this subject, you're going to cause a great deal of pain which we are not going to be able to accommodate. (*Pause.*) If we in this country, in the First World, were to ask these questions of the Colombians, we could cause a mass psychosis.

(*Silence.*)

(*Subdued.*) I'm going to bed.

(*He begins to go off. He stops and turns to HELEN.*)

I had an idea.

(*Silence.*)

For Gustavo's plastic for his father.

(*Pause.*)

A globe. A world! Make him a world!

(*HELEN lifts her head with a look of hope. CHARLES goes off.*

Blackout.)

part two

scene one

Late evening.

The Waldergraves have had their meal with the Escobars.

There are coffee cups around the place and maybe a cheeseboard. This latter could be on the book-shelf. There may also be side-plates, wine-glasses, an empty bottle or two etc. There are coats on the hanger. On the floor has been left a large translucent ball.

The room lights are off. There is only light coming from off which shines on the ball and makes it luminous. On the bookshelf, provocatively displayed, is the novel One Hundred Years of Solitude *by Gabriel Garcia Marquez.*

After a moment, HELEN rushes on. She is wearing a nightdress. She is wiping her face as if she has been caught in the middle of washing it.

She suddenly stops and turns.

HELEN: Stay away!
> (*CHARLES comes on. He is in his vest. Both CHARLES and HELEN show signs of having drunk too much.*)
CHARLES: What?!
HELEN: I don't want to hear it! Stay away! I'm not one of your pupils! Especially as you're in the wrong!
> (*CHARLES stands in silence. HELEN sits on the sofa and puts her head into the towel in her hands. Silence. CHARLES paces. He puts the light on.*)
> Turn it off!
> (*CHARLES turns the light off. Silence. CHARLES seems unable to find the right words to say.*)
> Go on! Why don't you say it? I let you down in front of the middle-classes again. Is that all that's important to you? Well I can tell you, it's better than you behaving like a servant! You'd think he was the king of Colombia. I didn't

think I'd see the day when the great liberal Waldergrave
would be so overwhelmed by the fat hand of the rich.

CHARLES: (*Ironically.*) It's cultural nervousness!

HELEN: O, well, then the pig must be uncultured because
HE wasn't nervous!

CHARLES: Don't try and deflect the argument. And keep
your voice down!

HELEN: You've been servant to a pig!

CHARLES: Shut up! I'm angry for a very good reason!

HELEN: He was drunk! His wife had to carry him upstairs!

CHARLES: Don't play this game with me. You'd done
everything possible to embarrass me all evening...

HELEN: You?! Why're you making...why do you always
make things look like a personal attack on you?

CHARLES: If you attack my guests you attack me. And that's
(*Points to globe*) the best example. What else could I do?

HELEN: Aren't you attacking me now?

CHARLES: No.

HELEN: Yes you are!

CHARLES: I'm trying to show you the truth. To bring right
up to your face (*Puts a hand to her face.*) the reality (*She
pushes his hand away scornfully*) of this evening. I thought
when I asked Gustavo to go and get his plastic globe, this
thing he'd made for his father that it was the only way to
defuse what you'd turned into a powder-keg: with all your
insulting asides, innuendos, questions...

HELEN: Shut up!

CHARLES: No. We'll come to all that. Why should I have
to use that to defuse things? Why should I even NEED to
defuse anything?...

HELEN: Exactly! Why? What's wrong with wanting to know
what the rich man might think about his poor country?

CHARLES: Christ! In a few years Gustavo will be as rich as
Croesus! You wouldn't recognise him. He'll give even less
of a toss about his poor than we give about ours.

HELEN: I didn't say!...

(*CHARLES has circled the sofa and now stands behind it.*)

CHARLES: It's all shit! It doesn't mean anything to us because in the end it doesn't mean anything to them. If it did mean anything to them they wouldn't send their kids over here to be taught and if it did in some ultimate, ethical way mean something to us we wouldn't take them! And then I wouldn't teach them!

HELEN: Well if it means so little why're you making such a fuss?

CHARLES: Because, I'd even, to make things easier, warmer, been prepared to put myself on the line by praising myself in order that the plastic feast about to be presented would be all the more creditable, tasty, all the more a victory for the forces of reason over those...

(*He paces unable to find words.*)

I'm a Geography teacher! Escobar says...

HELEN: The pig.

CHARLES: Shut up! He says when his son brings it on: what is it? (*Pause.*) 'the fourth world'! What: like a globe, an atlas, a map? Yes! So where are all the countries? Me, red-faced, geographer, what can I say? Well that's bad enough! But then his explanation...

HELEN: It was a beautiful idea and you'd admit that if you really wanted to face things. It's the only future, that's all he was saying: no first world, no second world or third world, only a fourth world.

CHARLES: It wasn't beautiful, it was meaningless!

HELEN: (*Angrily.*) You know that's not true! You're only saying it because you can't bear to face up to the fact that it showed deep sensitivity.

CHARLES: He said the problems of Colombia can't be solved until you take Colombia away from the Colombians! What's sensitive...

HELEN: And also for the whole world! That's what he said! No countries. That shows, also, deep understanding. You should rejoice! It was your idea! You inspired it!

CHARLES: (*Taking up an aggressive pose.*) No! (*Pause.*) Let me tell you the worst part of it all. Everybody could see it! Jesus, we've been over this so many times...I can even put up with a bit of flirting but this was almost a conspiracy! I

don't know whether you seduced him or he seduced you
or whether it was only…
(*HELEN suddenly jumps up and raises a fist to his face.*)
HELEN: You're going too far! I'm warning you.
(*CHARLES is stunned and hurt. He turns away.*)
CHARLES: You want to hit me! I'm the one who's been
offended! It's clear that Gustavo was enjoying your attack
on his father. You see? You've opened a door you're not
going to be able to close!
HELEN: What door?
CHARLES: You're giving him a view of his country that
he can't take home with him – if, in fact, Colombia is the
kind of place you say it is.
HELEN: I can't follow you! It's too late!
CHARLES: This seduction! This opening up of the channels
of the intellect as if it were to liberate him. This sharing of
information and ideas which is really the corrupting of an
innocent! And I warned you against it! What surprises me
is how he knows so much. When he arrived he clearly was
an innocent!
(*Silence.*)
HELEN: I didn't tell Gustavo anything and he didn't tell me
anything. I got it from the Amnesty Report!
(*Pause. CHARLES looks baffled for an instant.*)
CHARLES: Well that's even worse!
HELEN: Why?
CHARLES: Why? Because now you HAVE told him! And in
my house!
HELEN: I don't want to go on with this, it's going to end up
with a fight.
CHARLES: OK! Alright! Then what about this?
HELEN: What?
(*He indicates the Marquez book.*)
CHARLES: What's the purpose of putting a book like this in
such a provocative position?
HELEN: A book like what? How do you know what kind of
book it is? Nobody mentioned it and you said you'd never
read it!

CHARLES: You put it there to provoke something. Either
Escobar would be interested in discussing it because he's
Colombian, in which case I'm in the shit because I haven't
read it! Or he would deliberately ignore it because of its
provocative content.

HELEN: He's provocative!

CHARLES: Which is what he did!…

HELEN: Offensive and therefore provocative. He is a pig and
when he lashed his belly to our table, I'd had enough!…

CHARLES: Christ! (*He goes to the light switch.*) Suppose he is
offensive! So what? What difference does that make?

HELEN: (*Astounded.*) What!

(*CHARLES turns light on.*)

Turn it off!

(*CHARLES returns to the bookcase and the Marquez.*)

Turn the light off!

(*She gets up.*)

CHARLES: Why?

HELEN: I don't want it on!

(*CHARLES opens the book.*)

CHARLES: (*He reads aloud.*) 'Many years later, as he faced the
firing squad, Colonel Aureliano…' – There you are!

(*HELEN turns the light off and puts the globe on the bookshelf
in a position that would make its being lit by the light off
plausible.*)

Fascist!

(*HELEN returns to sofa.*)

HELEN: No, I want the light off so I can watch Gustavo's
world glow!

CHARLES: It's there in the first line of the book! How to
welcome guests from Colombia. Let them read about firing
squads! How to have your Colombian child educated: in
a house where you KNOW they read about Colombian
execution!

HELEN: Yes! It's easy to understand why they wouldn't
want Gustavo to read the book! Not because it's about sex
but because it's about politics! Isn't that stupid! Drawing
Gustavo's attention to the book for the only reason that
might encourage him to look into it. If they'd banned it for

being political NOBODY would want to read it. I think people who are that stupid are dangerous.

CHARLES: Nobody's said they banned the book!

HELEN: Nobody's said they kill orchestra conductors!

CHARLES: (*Bewilderedly.*) What!

(*Silence. CHARLES shakes his head with disbelief and goes off. HELEN lights a cigarette aggressively. A moment later, CHARLES returns with a bottle and clean glasses. As he comes on he puts the light on. HELEN doesn't respond. CHARLES sits down. He pours a glass of wine for himself and HELEN. He hangs his head. He lights a cigarette tiredly.*)

To be honest, I'll be glad when they're gone; when he's gone: Gustavo. When the whole thing is over.

HELEN: What thing? Life? The world?

CHARLES: (*Gasps.*) The man was telling us about his holiday home on Cape Corrientes! Sipping. Not promiscuously gulping...

HELEN: He was drunk!

CHARLES: Not at the point I'm talking about.

HELEN: He just got more and more drunk!

CHARLES: Any other hostess would have discussed the menu: the paella and the pickled fish and the iced vegetable soup! And whether one would have preferred the Tarator soup. Might one have gone for a Sevillian salad? With Spanish corn on the side? Or maybe stuffed onions? Noodles with clams? Or a baked JEWfish?...

HELEN: No! Looking at him: his huge rich, pigness, opened my eyes. I could see now how Gustavo is NOT his father's son.

(*CHARLES looks surprised.*)

That was one of the first things he told me: that he was adopted by Escobar. Just another one of the things you DIDN'T tell me...

CHARLES: You didn't tell me either!

HELEN: God if I had you'd have been...well you'd have probably sent him packing there and then for attempting to seduce me: stoking up my pity. Anyway, seeing this, I look deeper into the folds of the fat man's face. And then I remembered something YOU said. Remember? When you said about the justice minister not getting shot by the drugs people. Well in that report you gave me it said that most of those who've been shot are the poor or supporters of the poor. (*Pause.*) The pig Escobar is rich!

CHARLES: I wish I could tell you…if you could see how wrong you were, the damage you do – probably mostly to Gustavo – it's outrageous! You can't see it. If you could you'd experience deep shame.

(*Silence.*)

You see? Silence! What does that betoken? You're making my life intolerable! Can't you see that? And I'll tell you why: You have choices in this world and those choices face teachers the same as anyone else. If one wants to go on teaching you have to please the hand that feeds you.

(*There is a gasp of outrage from HELEN.*)

Gasp as much as you like! It's true! And I notice you don't turn down the perks! Your little flirtations. You're worried about shanty towns in Bogota, what about the shanty towns in London? What about the people living off rubbish tips in Cheshire? Or is it perhaps less poignant for being less romantic? Less Latin-blooded? Less mestizo and castanets? Eh? I might have students from China! From Turkey! From Iran! What are you going to say if their parents visit? And what if they invite us to visit them, which in the case of China might be quite nice?

(*Silence. HELEN looks outraged and furious.*)

HELEN: OK. I've had enough of this. Thousands of people have disappeared in Colombia which might not bother you, but if it doesn't, you're sick.

(*She gets up. She takes the Amnesty Report from beneath a cushion on the sofa. She occasionally reads from the piece of paper.*)

Did I tell you that (*Reads*) the conductor of the Medellin Symphony Orchestra was shot? (*Stops reading.*) The death squads advertise – they put hit-lists in the newspapers – that's probably why Gustavo was reading *The Sun*: to see how far OUR papers have gone down that road… On those lists have been (*Reads*) a former foreign minister and

other political leaders – usually LIBERALS and those on
the left: journalists and trade union leaders. There are a
hundred and forty different death squads! (*Pause.*) But listen
to this: in Medellin, the head of the TEACHER'S union
was shot dead!
(*Silence.*)
Are you moved by that? That's why I said to him about
our unions. (*Pause. She reads.*) The National Teacher's Union
presented the Procurator General with a list of over three
hundred teachers who'd been threatened with death since
July and because of this, because of this complaint, fifteen
of them have been killed. (*Stops reading.*) Teachers! Fifteen
teachers have been (*Refers to paper*) ...liquidated!
(*Silence.*)
I told you, when it's not teachers being killed, i.e. those
who, you could argue, give a voice to the poor, it's the
poor themselves. And maybe what worries Gustavo is that
his father is RICH. Maybe he's frightened that his father is
implicated.

CHARLES: Implicated?

HELEN: Yes! And that's it for me: the bottom line. My worry.
My horror. My...I want to know whether we, in this house,
the house of a teacher, have been entertaining a murderer
of teachers! (*Pause.*) BECAUSE I COULDN'T LIVE
WITH THAT!
(*Pause.*)

CHARLES: Helen, you answer the question in the absurd
sound of the words as you ask it. All you're really saying is:
he – Gustavo – could, if he wanted to, seduce you with his
vulnerability.
(*CHARLES gets up. He goes off. He turns the light off as he
goes. HELEN bites her knuckle. She gets up. She picks up the
book. She reads from the beginning.*)

HELEN: 'Many years later, as he faced the firing squad,
Colonel Aureliano Buendia was to remember that distant
afternoon when his father took him to discover ice.'
(*Pause.*)
(*Thoughtfully.*) '...to discover ice.'!

103

(*Silence. HELEN shuts the book and replaces it. She stands still
and silent and looks off to the light. HELEN goes to the coats on
the hanger. She pauses. She begins to go through the pocket of the
coat. CHARLES comes into the light. CHARLES comes slowly
towards her. HELEN is deeply into the rifling. As she pulls out
a wallet or pocket-book, CHARLES speaks.*)

CHARLES: So.

(*HELEN jumps with a gasp.*)

I don't know whether what I'm going to say will get across
to you...

(*Silence. CHARLES is looking for words.*)

(*Slowly, menacingly.*) The ethos and curriculum of the true
Britisher – the Englander, was built on his cuckoo instinct
to colonise. Which is not something to be proud of but
it's a fact. Only, it's not quite like that. Because the likes
of me have implanted into that curriculum, something
to clip the wings of the cuckoo. What we call: cause for
concern. (*Pause.*) Cause for concern. (*Pause.*) Go back to
William Wilberforce, and you'll see how he, in this society
which created the First World fought to denounce the
slavery it also created; and because of people like him,
you'll find people like me who are active in our cause for
concern. (*Pause.*) No matter what you say about Colombia,
about what happens in some spurned and maybe squalid
corner of the Third World, our relationship with them
– all of those countries – is good and works because we
– leaders, ethically of the First World, have embedded like
a constitutional clause in our curriculum that we have the
capacity for and show cause for concern. (*Pause.*) Now...
(*Pause.*) I can – because, maybe, I accept that there's
something wrong with our relationship: that you don't love
me; that you don't respect me et cetera, et cetera; that you
don't trust me or have faith in me – I can understand why
you may not have faith and be able to trust the things I
say, and how you may think I don't know what I speak of
when I speak of a cause for concern or you may simply
not know what I speak of though I DO! That doesn't
matter. It doesn't matter because when it comes to issues

like this, I'm not important. WE are not important! What's important... (*Pause*) What's important... (*He holds up the wallet.*) ...is this. (*Pause*) For all your spurious caring for justice and whether wrongs are righted or whether we see in the right or wrong place, wrong from right – this (*Waving wallet.*) is an act of colonialism! An act of colonialism in our house! You've gone into this jacket and that's the same as going into the state of Colombia, without permission and taken over... (*Waves wallet.*) The finance department, the foreign office, the ministry of the Interior, the department of agriculture, the department of technology, the secret service, in short, the whole bloody government! The government itself! Both branches – legislative and executive! (*He taps the wallet with his hand.*) And you did it for an infatuation; worse than that – you've fallen in love: with one of my pupils! That's unforgivable! Who knows how far you've gone...

HELEN: Liar! Open it! I want to know whether the pig IS implicated!

CHARLES: Implicated! In what?

HELEN: The death squads!

CHARLES: That is such a terrible thing to say. (*Pause.*) It's got the basic intuitive cruelty of the child cutting a worm into pieces and watching it squirm.
(*Silence.*)
I am not going to open this. (*Waves wallet.*) This will not happen in my house.

HELEN: I only wanted to know! Who is that being cruel to?

CHARLES: (*Suddenly losing control.*) Me, you bastard, me!
(*Silence. GUSTAVO comes on timidly in dressing gown. He seems afraid to speak. The three look at each other in silence.*)

CHARLES: What?

GUSTAVO: (*Fearfully.*) I heard my father. He...he said he is very angry.
(*CHARLES looks horrified.*)
He said...I think you say...humble.

CHARLES: Humiliated.

GUSTAVO: He said...

(*CHARLES shouts as if he's hoping that Escobar will hear and things can be retrieved.*)

CHARLES: I don't want to hear anymore! Are you happy about this?

GUSTAVO: (*Tearfully.*) No! No, I am not.

(*GUSTAVO hurries off.*)

CHARLES: (*Shouting after GUSTAVO.*) No! Exactly! Get to bed!

(*CHARLES advances on HELEN.*)

(*Threateningly.*) You...you...I'll tell you once more as I'll tell you again and again though I may know that no light will ever shine in there. (*Points to her head.*) Whatever is peculiar to Colombia is peculiar to it. Just as whatever is peculiar to Britishness is peculiar to being British. IT'S NOT OUR FAULT! And the peculiarities of the Colombians, are very much conditioned by the fact that it's in the Third World! By the fact, for example, that voters in America who vote for a President have more power in Colombia than those voters who vote for Colombia's President. Not only is it not their fault, it's almost cruel to make any other kind of judgement about them! (*Short pause.*) It's ironic that your infatuation has caused this distress: not only for the Escobars and for me, but for him too: Gustavo, the object of it.

(*CHARLES puts wallet in jacket and takes jacket off with him. HELEN collapses onto sofa in despair. Blackout.*)

scene two

Next day.

CHARLES is sitting glumly on the sofa. The globe has been left on the floor as if discarded.

HELEN comes on. She's dressed for outdoors. She carries bag of shopping which she puts down. She looks at CHARLES worriedly.

HELEN: Did you excuse me?

CHARLES: (*Grumpily.*) Did you get the paper?

(*He sits.*)

HELEN: I'm sorry, Charlie. What else can I say?

(*Pause. She looks in the bag for the paper.*)

I just couldn't face them. Were they alright?

CHARLES: They were alright. Give me the paper Helen. I need to look at the match report.

(*She finds the paper. She sits nervously on the edge of the sofa, still in her coat. She looks frail and uncomfortable. She gives CHARLES the broadsheet newspaper which he almost snatches from her. HELEN hangs her head. She gets up. She begins to fold up the Indian blanket slowly.*)

HELEN: I feel so stupid. I am stupid! I feel so ashamed and miserable. It's as if I've got a hangover for being drunk on stupidity. I let Gustavo get so far into my mind! I couldn't even say goodbye to his parents! And you're the one who has to teach him. (*Pause.*) Charles?

(*CHARLES continues reading.*)

We'll have to change things for the future. It mustn't happen again. (*Pause.*) Even if I'd been right I had no right looking into things that don't concern me!

(*She suddenly sits.*)

That's what it is.

(*She goes to him and touches him tentatively.*)

It won't happen again. I'm sorry.

(*CHARLES looks up blankly and stares before him as though she wasn't there. He drops the paper to the floor. Silence. GUSTAVO looks on tentatively. He carries the* Ulysses *book. HELEN sees him. GUSTAVO looks uncomfortable.*)

Gustavo!

(*Suddenly, both she and CHARLES come to life.*)

(*Matronly.*) Gustavo, where were you at breakfast? You know it's a condition of you staying here!

(*GUSTAVO looks shocked. HELEN tidies a few things up.*)

If you behave like a child you'll have to be treated like one. We could always put you in a room on the campus.

CHARLES: Yes!

HELEN: I'm just saying Gustavo that you're treated specially, with special indulgence here. You should appreciate that!

CHARLES: (*Bitterly.*) Do you like football? Spanish types do don't they? Eh? What do you make of this?
(*He picks up paper.*)
Listen! (*He reads from the paper.*) 'Like the Conquistadors or even a Task Force sent out by new-to-Spanish-Football-manager Dave Smith, the little-known but going-places Spanish side rocked City with a salvo of goals like a commando assault on Goose Green or a cavalry charge from Captain Pizarro's men as they conquered the local Inca Empire in this European tie.' (*Pause.*) 'As if the Spanish side took heart from Keats' eagle-eyed Cortez, "silent on a peak in Darien", an early reference to the calm of the first half before the storm of small arms fire about to rage, the play seemed almost immobile, bogged down in the muddy trench-warfare of a game of British football with all the quintessential elements: wind, rain and mud.'
(*CHARLES shakes his head with disbelief.*)
(*Reading.*) 'Like a clutch of cowardly Argentinians before Stanley or a cackle of bewildered Indians in some Andean valley, the local side sunk into the mud of retreat as Gonzalez – one of the Spaniards' big guns, opened fire from on high at the edge of the box in the 56th minute. Goalkeeper MONTEZUMA Smith! (*Shakes his head.*) couldn't have even guessed at the HISTORICAL implications of the volley from the Old World that struck the back of the net with a resounding wallop that would echo down the centuries.'
(*Silence. CHARLES looks at GUSTAVO.*)
GUSTAVO: I am sorry. I didn't understand.
CHARLES: You won! The Spaniards won! Beat us at our own game. (*Pause.*) But I bet you haven't got such a command of English. (*Pause.*) You only won the football Gustavo! So between now and the time you go, just be on your best behaviour!
(*Silence. GUSTAVO looks upset.*)
GUSTAVO: (*Tentatively.*) I...I brought the book.
(*HELEN goes to him quickly.*)
CHARLES: What book?

HELEN: I shouldn't have given it to you.

CHARLES: What book?

(*HELEN takes the book and goes to put it in her shopping bag.*)

HELEN: It's just a book I leant Gustavo.

CHARLES: Come on, Helen!

HELEN: It's *Ulysses*, Charles! You wouldn't have read it!

CHARLES: (*Surprised.*) *Ulysses*? By James Joyce! I didn't think anybody could read that. It's got no punctuation has it?

(*He puts his hand out. HELEN gives him the book.*)

Go on then, Gustavo!

(*GUSTAVO goes. CHARLES turns to the back of the book where the marker is. He reads.*)

For Christ's sake Helen! What do you think you're up to!

(*HELEN turns away ashamedly.*)

You've even underlined it! (*He reads aloud*.) 'I'll put on my best shift and drawers. Let him have a good eyeful out of that to make his micky stand for him. I'll let him know if that's what he wanted: that his wife is fucked...'! You didn't let him read this! It's the last straw Helen! Haven't I told you? To educate you have to BE educated! In fact, it's probably the case that you need to be educated in order to be ABLE to be educated! (*Pause.*) I feel as if I've had my insides taken out – no, my brain! The lining of my brain spread out on the floor of the bathroom and smeared with...with (*Nastily.*) Your excrement. Your peasant, stupid, thick-fingered, pop-eyed, incest-bred excrement!

(*CHARLES storms off. HELEN sits on the sofa wrapping her arms around her in despair. Blackout.*)

scene three

Later.

HELEN is sitting despondently on the sofa. She is still wearing her outdoor clothes. She is staring blankly at the floor. She smokes a cigarette.

GUSTAVO comes on slowly and quietly. He wears a track-suit. HELEN ignores his presence. GUSTAVO takes the globe from the shelf.

Silence.

GUSTAVO: I thought…maybe we can play game. Another game.
(*Silence.*)
Football!
(*He suddenly drops the globe onto his foot, gives it a gentle kick and begins dribbling it around the room.*)
HELEN: (*Horrified.*) Gustavo! Stop it!
GUSTAVO: You see! In Colombia if you can play football, you have already won the goal. You can do whatever you want to and no one will harm you. It is the same here? I think so! You know: ENGLAND! ENGLAND! ENGLAND!
HELEN: STOP IT!
(*Silence.*)
GUSTAVO: OK. So we set up game. Yes? You are one team and you want to score goal with me and I am team to score goal with you. This way we play what we really mean is: if YOU score goal with me, you are into my family and my home and if I score goal with you, I am with YOUR family. OK? (*Short pause.*) Isn't that why you want them to visit so that maybe you can one day visit them?
(*Silence.*)
OK!
(*GUSTAVO bounces globe. HELEN looks away.*)
So first thing we kick off. Who to kick off? We toss coin.
(*He takes out coin.*)
I call tails.
(*He tosses. He reads coin.*)
It is heads so you win! You kick off!
(*He tries to goad her into playing by pushing globe against her feet. He steps back and stands crouching like a goalie.*)
You get to kick at my goal if you answer question right. OK? (*Pause.*) If you want to be in my family, why'd you pretend to be my friend? OK?
(*Silence.*)

OK! Silence! Then it becomes my go. I kick at your goal.
Now you ask ME question.
(*Silence.*)
OK. Then I give you answer to mine. (*Pause.*) Because...
because you are English. Because you are rulers and tell
us what to do! Because you are not believable! Because
you don't care whether you are with me or in my family or
ANYthing! You don't care. About nothing! I answer right!
Now I can score goal!
(*GUSTAVO kicks ball angrily towards HELEN. HELEN
jumps up.*)

HELEN: (*Beside herself.*) I'm sick to death! I'm telling you. Get
out! Stay away from me! Don't speak to me unless you
have to! Just do things as you're meant to! As you would if
you were home.

GUSTAVO: (*Angrily though not disrespectfully.*) Why do you
speak to me like this? I am not a child!

HELEN: O, I know that! You're much too clever! You thought
you could worm your way into my family so you made
yourself look vulnerable like a child. All this stuff about
wanting to be a vet! All I wanted to do was help you. Help
you get on with your father. But now, when I look back to
that meal and think how you were using me... You'll be
gone in a few days Gustavo so just stay away from me until
then!

GUSTAVO: (*Tearfully.*) If I did want to be in your family ask
why! No! It's I am the one who tried to protect you!
(*HELEN looks angry and perplexed and hurt. GUSTAVO goes.
HELEN goes to the door. She shouts after GUSTAVO.*)

HELEN: Stay away from me, Gustavo, until you go! Don't
speak to me unless you have to! Just do things as you're
meant to! As you would if you were home!
(*Silence. She goes off. She returns to stab and puncture the ball
but it just slips off. She collapses onto the ball and laughs until
she cries and has to wipe away tears.
Blackout.*)

scene four

Night.

The light is off. The globe is on the bookshelf glowing.

HELEN is in her nightdress. She is sitting on the sofa with her feet tucked beneath her. The Marquez book Love In The Time of Cholera *is standing on the bookshelf with its cover towards her. She is looking at the book in silence.*

CHARLES comes on. He's been out. He puts the light on.

CHARLES: Hiya Helen.
HELEN: (*Turning to him. Subdued.*) Hiya Charles.
    (*Without taking his coat off, CHARLES sits next to her. He puts a hand on her knee.*)
CHARLES: Not sad are you?
HELEN: No. Why should I be?
CHARLES: Is he in bed?
HELEN: Yes.
CHARLES: I can't say I'm sorry he's going.
    (*He pecks her. He takes his coat off.*)
    I'll turn the light off. So you can look at Gustavo's world.
HELEN: You don't need to.
CHARLES: It's alright.
    (*CHARLES turns the light off. He stands a little awkwardly with his hands in his pockets. As he speaks, he looks at the globe.*)
    (*Teacherly. Enthusiastically.*) Gustavo's right. What we need is a new world. Tomorrow. See, it's not just the duty of the thinking man to look for answers to the questions but a part of his freedom. Without his thought the seas will mutiny. But...what do we do about the world? The US created the Third World. After World War Two. As part of its projected world order. The idea was to create parts of the world where you can encourage repressive regimes, then when the people rise up you can say it's a Soviet plot and then you have a clear, identifiable enemy for your own malcontents to worry about! And you can do extraordinary things in those places because it's not part of our world. It's

another world. A Third World! It's a very evil imperialism,
Helen, that can create the anarchy of the death squads in
order to have a political vacuum to exploit. That's what
the Third World is. And then the Yankee poses as a father
figure – a patroniser more like. (*Pause.*) Ha! The President
of the United States is helping Colombia clean out its drug
barons. But why? Not because he cares about Colombia
but because babies who have died from the drugs in the
blood of the mother are being buried in boxes just around
the corner from the White House. His good Christian
rectitude has been severely affronted by this burial ground
on the borders of his lawn. And if by chance rather
than sincere design he stops the drug trade and solves a
domestic problem of his own, what's he going to do when
the Colombian peasants who grow the dope rise up against
this new scenario which has left them destitute on their
mountain-sides? Simple: he'll call it communism and that'll
give him an excuse to send in his own death squads!
(*HELEN looks at him with sadness.*)
I know. You're worrying about what Gustavo's going
back to. But as his teachers, we have to allow him to be
responsible for what he knows. You agree with that don't
you?

HELEN: Was that in the Amnesty report?

CHARLES: O, no. (*Pause.*) Helen?

HELEN: Yes?

CHARLES: You agree don't you?

HELEN: Yes.

(*He smiles and kisses her.*)

CHARLES: I'm off. I'm whacked. A big night. We discussed
so much I can hardly remember what we said.
(*He leans over the back of the sofa and gives her a kiss.*)
Night. (*Pause.*) I love you.

HELEN: Night. I'll be up in a minute.

(*CHARLES goes. Silence. After a moment or two she gets up
and takes book from shelf. She sits on edge of sofa. She looks at
book and strokes its cover etc. She gets up, puts book down and
goes off. After a moment, she comes back on with some wrapping*)

paper, cord etc. She begins to wrap up the book. After a few more moments, as she's finishing the wrapping, GUSTAVO comes on. He is naked with a robe wrapped around him.)

GUSTAVO: (*Quietly. Tentatively.*) Charles has gone to his room. (*Silence. It must be clear that HELEN is aware of his nakedness.*) Why did you want to see me? Why did you want Charles to be in bed?

HELEN: I don't know. I'm not sure. I feel freer. Freer to understand.

GUSTAVO: Isn't it over?

HELEN: I've been used. Until I find out why, it's never over.

GUSTAVO: Used?

HELEN: Yes! By you! (*Pause.*) Gustavo! I like you a lot, you know that. But you deceived me. You made me look like an idiot! That's a terrible thing to do. Especially as you knew I was vulnerable. I understood YOUR vulnerability and you took advantage of mine! If you can do that to somebody, if you can deceive them it means you feel NOTHING for them. That's what made me feel so awful! Can't you see that? I'm talking about trust which is something maybe they don't have in Colombia. I DID feel for you, and tried to help you emotionally. (*Pause.*) You know that.

GUSTAVO. But I don't know what you mean.

HELEN: Yes you do! You knew if I got involved with your problem – if it was a problem – about wanting to be a vet, that eventually I'd get more involved. I suppose your intention was to...I don't know what or why, maybe you think you can be readopted over here but it's got nothing to do with wanting to be a vet. You made that quite clear the night you came in here kicking that globe around. And then...

GUSTAVO: But...

HELEN: Wait a minute. Then I ask myself: why should the problem YOU'RE having with YOUR father be any different from the problem anyone else has with THEIR father? It's no different. (*Scornfully.*) Unless it's that he dresses up as a cowboy!

GUSTAVO: No you are wrong! Because everyone in Colombia especially like my father wants to play like a child.

HELEN: Well I can understand that because you've got a very good ability for appearing childlike and innocent!

GUSTAVO: No! I am not a child. And I don't want to be innocent. But in Colombia everyone and especially my father wants to be innocent. So if everyone is innocent, everyone is innocent of the death squads. And if no one is guilty of them they don't exist. Are YOU guilty? Is it the same here. Does everybody here want to be innocent. So that they can say that things don't exist? My father dresses as a cowboy. And then the cowboys go off to play games with their guns like children who are innocent. But I am NOT innocent!

(*Silence.*)

HELEN: (*With a sigh.*) OK, Gustavo. (*Pause.*) You'll be gone tomorrow. I hope you learned something. Here.

(*She hands him the parcel.*)

GUSTAVO: What is it?

HELEN: It's a book. By your Colombian. It's called: *Love in the Time of Cholera.*

(*GUSTAVO looks dumbfounded.*)

GUSTAVO: You hope that I have learned? But you have learned nothing!

HELEN: (*Shocked.*) You can't talk to me like that!

GUSTAVO: Yes! Because it's too late for you to pretend you are the teacher. You don't know. I know! You see, if I open this at home…

(*He draws his hand across his neck on a cut-throat gesture.*)

Perhaps at the customs…

HELEN: (*Angrily.*) That's not true!

GUSTAVO: I know that I know because I have seen how dangerous it is to know. Do you understand what I mean? No! To you it is only a book. A story. But in Colombia it is education. In Colombia, those who teach are killed. You know this. In my town. (*He is beginning to cry.*) This is why I don't want to go home even though I know I must. Why don't you believe me? If you learn in Colombia you become guilty. Then they kill you. You know so they kill you. Like they wanted to kill me.

HELEN: You?!

(*Silence. GUSTAVO suddenly snatches the bottle from the bookcase and drinks deeply from it.*)

Wait! Let me get you a glass.

(*HELEN rushes off. GUSTAVO breathes deeply, nervously. He flexes his muscles as if he doesn't know he's doing it. HELEN returns with a glass. She fills it for GUSTAVO in silence. GUSTAVO drinks as if it were forbidden.*)

GUSTAVO: Ariel Pabon Pabon was my friend. You see, when he died... (*Overcome.*)

(*Silence. He drinks.*)

He was my age. His father was a teacher. His mother was a good woman. She always helped. (*Pause.*) He was coming home from school. Just near his home. So near. A red chevrolet pick-up truck stopped. Three men got out and forced Ariel into the truck. (*Pause.*) It is KNOWN that they were policemen. (*Pause.*) His body was found an hour later. When he was found, his wrists were tied with shoelaces and a leather strap. His hands were swollen and his nails were black. He had six... (*He breaks down.*)

(*Silence. HELEN pours drinks. They drink.*)

He had six bullets in his head and one in his back. They had burned his hands and his hair and his teeth were broken. (*Pause.*) He had been kicked and beaten and... (*Cries.*) It was known that it was the police because a pair of pinchers...these (*He gestures to describe the action of the use of a pair of pliers*) these used to pull things... (*Pause*) which belonged to the police...was found near the body. Ariel... (*Pause. Cries.*) Ariel had lumps of flesh missing. They had been pulled out (*Cries*) with these...

(*GUSTAVO makes an exaggerated gesture describing the use of a pair of pliers. HELEN holds GUSTAVO.*)

HELEN: Gustavo!

GUSTAVO: It is the same here! The police protect the innocent. Only in Colombia, anyone guilty they kill. They

kill teachers, they kill students, they kill school children! I
know so they came to kill me!

HELEN: But Charles said you knew nothing!

(*GUSTAVO drinks.*)

GUSTAVO: And that is what you believe. You see? I told you
I protected you.

HELEN: What do you mean?

(*HELEN drinks and refills glasses.*)

GUSTAVO: Before. Before the Escobars came. You were
arguing with Charles. You remember this? And it would be
worse if you knew so I didn't tell you. Worse for you. I was
standing over there.

HELEN: Gustavo, you will tell me!

GUSTAVO: And if I tell you?...

HELEN: Make me guilty too!

(*GUSTAVO drinks.*)

GUSTAVO: I saw my mother...I can't say this...

(*HELEN holds GUSTAVO.*)

HELEN: You must!

(*Silence. GUSTAVO drinks again.*)

GUSTAVO: The police came for me. But my mother. My real
mother. Maria Alvarado. They killed...

(*He suppresses his tears. Silence.*)

HELEN: Gustavo. (*Pause.*) Did Charles know that you saw
this?

GUSTAVO: Yes.

HELEN: God!

(*Pause.*)

GUSTAVO: My father, my step-father Escobar. He is
a policeman. He is a...you know...special? Secret
policeman?

(*Pause.*)

Charles knew.

(*Silence.*
Blackout.)

scene five

Later. Middle of night.

GUSTAVO is laying on top of HELEN, between her legs. It's ambiguous. Not necessarily in the position of intercourse; perhaps as if he were a child sleeping on his mother.

She is holding him to her. They are asleep. His dressing gown has been taken off and is draped over them.

CHARLES comes on. He pauses and looks at them. He sits on the sofa and watches them for at least half a minute in silence.

At the end of this time, CHARLES gets up and gently takes GUSTAVO's dressing gown from his back, revealing the boy's nakedness. He pauses for a moment. He carefully tiptoes from the two and hangs GUSTAVO's gown on the hanger. As he puts the gown on the hanger he suddenly relaxes as if relieved of a great tension.

He pauses.

CHARLES goes off.

Blackout.

End.

MANIFEST DESTINY
(an opera libretto)

Characters

DANIEL
a British Jewish composer

LEILA
a Palestinian Muslim poetess, his lover

MOHAMMED
a Palestinian suicide bomber

OMAH
a Palestinian suicide bomber

MRS PRESIDENT HILLARY
of the US

MR DIRECTOR
of the CIA

JAILER
Guantanamo Bay

Manifest Destiny was first produced as a benefit performance for the Guantanamo Human Rights Commission at the Tricycle Theatre, London on Sunday 27 June 2004 with the following singers:

Bernadette Lord, *Soprano*

Alexander Anderson-Hal, *Tenor*

James McOran-Campbell, *Baritone*

Peter Willcock, *Baritone*

Composer, Keith Burstein

Libretto, Dic Edwards

Artwork, Ralph Steadman

Director, Gari Jones

ACT ONE: IMAGES

Scene 1

London. The near future. The flat of DANIEL XAVIER, composer.

DANIEL is sitting bolt upright. He has recently gone blind, a response to trauma and as his physical sight has faded so his inner sight has intensified into a vision of the terrible and strange events sweeping the world.

DANIEL
> O Israel!
> Long since you fell to Sharon,
> destroyer of Shabra and Shatilla,
> destroyer of light.
> Your covenant betrayed
> and all your flowers
> of love defiled.
>
> O America!
> torn by corruption
> the money terrorists
> have stolen the election!
> With a quarrel over ballot papers
> deleted the power of your people.
> Now the oil barons of New England
> are stalking your streets
> your forlorn stolen streets
> and in the world
> there is a darkness falling!

The poet, LEILA, his lover and partner, comes in. DANIEL looks at her, fearfully, in silence. She has been writing him a libretto, but has already joined a suicide cell.

LEILA
> You've been crying.

DANIEL

    I don't want you to leave.

LEILA

    I must fight for truth
    in the coming night.

DANIEL

    If you fight you'll die!

LEILA

    The beat of my heart
    is nothing compared with
    the Word in the people's hearts.

DANIEL

    And you will kill! And you will kill!

LEILA

    Yes, I will kill.
    We live in a hall of death
    filled with our butchered young!

DANIEL

    Then spare theirs!

LEILA

    O Daniel!
    Our children are innocent!
    Theirs are the offspring of the guilty

DANIEL

    What are you saying?

LEILA

    I have my father's work to do!

DANIEL

    Leila! I need you here!

LEILA

    I am poet of our world!
    They murdered my father

That is my poem;
my word is my weapon.

I am a child of the Third World
I am born in conflict
my mind is in conflict
my body is in conflict
I eat, breathe, drink, sleep
and study conflict
there is no peace in my day
in my soul, in my words
I must know why my
flowerless desert garden
carries the seed
of a Third World War.
I am the poet of the Arabian darkness
come to bring light.
I am a child of the Third World
I am born in conflict
my mind is in conflict
my body is in conflict

DANIEL holds onto her desperately.

DANIEL

Revenge is still-born!
Revenge is a treacherous lover!
My family died in the Nazi camps;
Silence became my poetry;

Then you woke my voice.
Please don't leave me.
Please don't shatter my dreams.

Now is the beginning
of my world, my night...
I must write,
Set my grief to music...
...don't go,
don't go.

LEILA

> I must fight for truth, I must fight for justice

DANIEL

> I love you

LEILA

> ...I love you...

LEILA leaves DANIEL. Both know they will never meet each other again.

Musical Interlude with film

DANIEL goes into the dark (lights down on him).

On a screen, a succession of images: leading up to the election of BUSH, and SHARON, 9/11, Afghanistan, Iraq...

DANIEL

> (*In between images.*)
> These? These? Are these the pictures
> to fill my darkness?
> She is gone, taken all her words
> I needed.
> I am silent, blind and lost!

We are the progeny of these images.

Silence.

Scene 2

Palestine. LEILA with the cell of suicide bombers.

They stand together serenely as though in prayer. Slowly and systematically they dress themselves and each other in the apparatus of suicide bombs.

ALL

> We will give our lives to fight
> will embrace martyrdom

will not be murdered
by First World power!
First world power.

LEILA

I am writing the poem
of our history
and will leave the shadow
of my life in the sky.

MOHAMMED

But you must first write your poem
to put the image of life
into your death.

OMAH

And my life.

ALL

Our death for life!
Our death for life!
Our death for life!
Our death for life!

OMAH

We love Death more than they love Life.

ALL

Our death for life!
Our death for life!
Our death for life!

OMAH

What we must do
may seem monstrous
but only in the moment.
They live for the day and
would steal our souls
to fuel their empty lives
and when their day is done, may die.
We cannot die in a moment
because our truth is eternal.

> We are truth's children.
> Remember: it is the child in the monster
> Who discovers the true meaning of ends.

LEILA

> ...the true meaning of ends.

ALL

> Our truth is eternal
> The truth is eternal
> Our death for life

LEILA

> and my life

OMAH

> and my life

MOHAMMED

> and my life.

ALL

> Our death for life!
> Our death for life!
> Our death for life!

OMAH

> We love Death more than they love Life.

ALL

> Our death for life!

MOHAMMED

> They stole the election
> and when the madman had won
> we were able to start
> what we have only begun.

> *OMAH straps a bomb to himself.*

OMAH

> They have betrayed their own values
> for their political Right
> to fight their mercenary fight!

He leaves.

LEILA gets up and begins to strap a bomb to herself.

ALL

> They cannot kill those prepared to die
> We'll break our wings to let us fly.

Exit OMAH.

Scene 3

MOHAMMED

> (*Stopping LEILA and pulling off her bomb.*)
> Not yet Leila, not yet!
> We need you to give
> the cause of our dying,
> the cause of our dying
> for those who live.

He holds LEILA.

> I have watched you Leila
> with growing surprise,
> so young yet so loving
> you have the world in your eyes.
> Your beautiful soul
> has rendered me weak
> you seem almost more precious
> than the freedom we seek.

MOHAMMED disarms LEILA. LEILA turns her back on him.

LEILA

> Why do you do this?
> Now I am confused:
> my passion is to fight
> but I fear you would use
> the fight to explore
> a more intimate passion.

MOHAMMED

> No! It is love, it is love.
> It is love.

LEILA

> I am confused:
> my passion is to fight...

MOHAMMED

> Does it matter if we fashion
> a private peace
> from this public war?

LEILA

> ...but you want something more.

LEILA / MOHAMMED

> It is love. It is love. It is love.
> It is love. It is love. It is love.

LEILA

> This is not what I foresaw!
> I will go to the mountains
> of Afghanistan
> and look to my soul
> to find the God in Man.

LEILA leaves.

MOHAMMED

> This pain is too real!
> Greater than all the grief of Islam.
> She'll be betrayed
> by the very thing she is.
> Her love of ideals is not an ideal for love,
> My love for her cannot let her die.
> Please don't leave me, please don't shatter my strength.
> Leila, your selflessness may lead you to perform acts
> against the very truth of your own pulsing life.
> I will follow you. I will follow you

to the mountains and bring you the peaceful truth of
        Islam
to rediscover your destiny in the heart of Man

...I love Life more than I love Death.

End of Act One.

ACT TWO: DANCE MUSIC

Scene 1

The White House: 'Viennese Waltz' (1)

MRS PRESIDENT and MR DIRECTOR of the CIA decamp from the White House Inauguration Ball to the Oval Office. They are drunk (with alcohol and power). MR DIRECTOR sees his chance to seduce MRS PRESIDENT with his grand stratagems of American dominion. From the distant ballroom, through the open door of the Oval Office, we hear the waltz music playing on into the early hours.

MRS PRESIDENT
> The Oval office!

MR DIRECTOR
> Sure looks great!

MRS PRESIDENT
> The Oval Office!

MR DIRECTOR
> Nice chintzy drapes!

MRS PRESIDENT
> The Oval Office!

MR DIRECTOR
> Cute Persian rugs!

MRS PRESIDENT
> The Oval Office!

MR DIRECTOR
> Needed a woman's touch! (*Caressing the President.*)
> …a woman's touch…a woman's touch
> So where do we begin, Mrs President?

MRS PRESIDENT
Begin what, Mr Director?

MR DIRECTOR
To kick Arabian ass!

MRS PRESIDENT
You mean...nine eleven?

MR DIRECTOR
Sure! That was a gift from God
So sweet I wish I'd been its architect.

MRS PRESIDENT
But what of the American dead?

MR DIRECTOR
Hey! More die on our roads!...

MRS PRESIDENT
O, the sadness of Highways,
O, the sadness of Highways...

MR DIRECTOR
...And with no kick-back.
So it's off to the Afghani desert!

MRS PRESIDENT
Where is that?

MR DIRECTOR
In Afghanistan!

MRS PRESIDENT
And where is Afghanistan?

MR DIRECTOR
Somewhere above Australia.

MRS PRESIDENT
And will the Australians mind?

MR DIRECTOR
Hell, they ain't Arabs!

MRS PRESIDENT
>And what about the world?

MR DIRECTOR
>What world?

MRS PRESIDENT
>The...um...globe.

MR DIRECTOR
>It's ours!
>That's all been figured out:
>and we got a patsy
>in Downing Street
>to soften up the doubters
>and the liberals
>and the moralists.
>It's all downhill, kid
>and you will become
>the first American Emperor.
>Official!
>It's our Manifest Destiny!

Scene 2

LEILA in Afghanistan / DANIEL in London.

LEILA
>So cold on this mountaintop
>the icy winds of American
>vengeance like Arctic waters
>like Arctic waters.
>O Daniel! I need your breath
>to warm my heart
>as I need your music
>to let me breathe.

DANIEL
>Blindness is not the dark,
>without colour there is only cold.

Blindness is like ice
I am surrounded by ice.

BOTH

Where are you?

LEILA

I need your music

DANIEL

Daughter of antiquity...

BOTH

O warm my heart...

LEILA

...to let me breathe

DANIEL

...mother of my words

BOTH

I need your breath to let me breathe

DANIEL

Mother of my words, my tunes are frozen.

LEILA

O Daniel I need your breath to warm my heart
As I need your music to let me breathe.

DANIEL

Daughter of antiquity, mother of my words
All my tunes are frozen.

LEILA

I need your breath...

BOTH

O warm my heart, O warm my heart,
O warm my heart!

Scene 3

Guantanamo: 'Tango' (1)

MOHAMMED is on his knees, blindfolded with his arms tied behind his back. He is bruised and bloody, his clothes soiled and torn. He has clearly been tortured for many hours.

MR DIRECTOR
> Shall we bugger you
> to save you?

MOHAMMED
> No need, sir! I am saved in your image!

MR DIRECTOR
> Shall we bugger you to confirm it?
> You Iraqi piece of shit.

MOHAMMED
> I'm Palestinian!

MR DIRECTOR
> That's worse!
> Totally buggerable!

MOHAMMED
> And now Christian
> Saved in your image!

MR DIRECTOR
> Then shall we bugger you anyway?
> You Iraqi piece of shit.

MOHAMMED
> No need, saintly one,
> You buggered all the Arabs long ago.
> I want now to be an American! To be an American!
> To be an American!

MR DIRECTOR
>And will you bugger other Arabs for us?
>enable us to bugger by proxy, to bugger by proxy,
>to bugger by proxy?
>You Iraqi piece of shit!

MOHAMMED is dragged away.

Scene 4

LEILA in Afghanistan, DANIEL in London.

LEILA
>For a century
>Western nations
>have brought terror
>to Arabia
>only because Arabia
>is where it is
>not because of what we've done.
>Before that century
>the Europeans killed American Indians
>to get their gold
>and make America great.
>Now America will kill Arabs
>to make Greater America.

>And we only want to live,we only want to live,
>We only want to live with the beauty of our beliefs.

Scene 5

Cross Rhythms

DANIEL in London, LEILA in Afghanistan, MR DIRECTOR and MOHAMMED in Guantanamo in an interrogation room. MOHAMMED is tied to a chair, blindfolded.

DANIEL

>My belief is in Leila's face
>redeemer of my memory.

LEILA

>This is an awful place
>brutaliser of my memory.

MR DIRECTOR

>(*To MOHAMMED.*)
>If yours is a valid race
>I will erase my very memory.

MOHAMMED

>(*To MR DIRECTOR.*)
>Let you and me embrace
>The New American Century.

DANIEL

>Leila, redeem my memory.

LEILA

>This is an awful place.

MR DIRECTOR

>I will erase my very memory.

MOHAMMED

>Let you and me embrace.

DANIEL

>Leila, redeemer of my memory.

LEILA

>This is an awful place!

DANIEL

>Memory!

LEILA

>Place!

MR DIRECTOR

>Memory!

ALL
> Embrace!

MOHAMMED
> I can give you
> a leading terrorist
> the voice of Al Qaeda
> the poet of the Arab revolution!

MR DIRECTOR
> Do it and we shall honour you
> with an audience with
> The President!

He helps MOHAMMED stand, takes off his blindfold and unties his hands, he leaves MOHAMMED.

MOHAMMED
> To be blind, to be blind,
> hidden from the light of evil
> comforted by the other
> evil of managed despair.
> We only wanted to live with the beauty of our beliefs.

DANIEL
> Leila, redeemer of my memory
> Daughter of antiquity and
> Mother of my words.
> Leila, redeem our love.

Scene 6

The White House: Viennese Waltz (2)

Some weeks later. MR DIRECTOR of the CIA holds a document he's brought for MRS PRESIDENT to sign.

MRS PRESIDENT
> I feel so uncertain.

MR DIRECTOR
    What's brought this on?

MRS PRESIDENT
    Am I being used?

MR DIRECTOR
    Used? By whom?

MRS PRESIDENT
    By you.

MR DIRECTOR
    By me?

MRS PRESIDENT
    What's your agenda?

MR DIRECTOR
    To beat 'em.

MRS PRESIDENT
    To beat who?

MR DIRECTOR
    The Arabs!

MRS PRESIDENT
    All Arabs?

MR DIRECTOR
    Sure! They're a pain in the neck.

MRS PRESIDENT
    Only a pain in the neck?

MR DIRECTOR
    Middle East is full of 'em.
    Shouldn't be there.
    Should be full of Israelis
    they are our friends.

MRS PRESIDENT
    I'm afraid for the children.
    I am a mother.

MR DIRECTOR
>Your kids are safe
>in Camp David.

MRS PRESIDENT
>Not my children!
>The children of Arabia!
>The children of Arabia!
>The children of Arabia!

MR DIRECTOR
>Mrs President,
>the Arabians have oil,
>natural resources,
>those resources belong to the world
>and we, on behalf of the world
>must rescue said resources...

MRS PRESIDENT
>Then it's not nine eleven?

MR DIRECTOR
>Nine eleven, whatever
>it doesn't matter.

MRS PRESIDENT
>I don't like it.

MR DIRECTOR
>This conflict will live
>beyond your term of office.
>It is our duty
>to resolve it.
>You will sign
>the authorisation!

MR DIRECTOR thrusts the document before MRS PRESIDENT.
She begins to sign it but she and MR DIRECTOR are surprised
by the sudden entry into the Oval Office of MOHAMMED who
is marched in by guards. He stumbles before them.

Scene 7

Tango (2)

MR DIRECTOR
> Mrs P, meet Mohammed. (*Hissed in her ear.*)
> Ain't that a great name? (*Out loud.*)

MRS PRESIDENT
> Is he a Muslim?

MR DIRECTOR
> Was, now a Christian
> convert to our values.

MRS PRESIDENT
> Our values, Mr Director?

MR DIRECTOR
> Yes! Profits not prophets.
> (*Aside.*) You Iraqi piece of shit.

MRS PRESIDENT
> And our philosophy?

MR DIRECTOR
> Action not thought.

MRS PRESIDENT
> And what of our stupid mistakes?

A set of images rapidly appears, including Castro's beard on fire.

MR DIRECTOR
> Duty before intelligence.
> Duty before intelligence
> Duty before in...

MRS PRESIDENT
> And what do you think Mohammed?

MR DIRECTOR
> (*Aside.*) You Iraqi piece of shit.

MOHAMMED
> Duty!

MRS PRESIDENT
> To Islam?

MOHAMMED
> To the American Dream!
> Take me to the Black Hills
> of Dakota, not the
> Hindu Kush not the
> Hindu Kush.

MRS PRESIDENT / MR DIRECTOR
> (*Together.*) Not the
> Hindu Kush!

MR DIRECTOR
> Conversion deluxe!
> This is the way to
> Full Spectrum Dominance!
> Pre-emptive strikes against everyone!

MRS PRESIDENT
> Against everyone?

MR DIRECTOR
> Everyone!

MRS PRESIDENT
> You mean,
> all Arabs?

MR DIRECTOR
> I mean... (*Shouting.*) ...everyone!
> The whole goddamn lot!

*Spitting and shouting at MRS PRESIDENT and MOHAMMED
who cling onto each other.*

Even our own
bums on the campuses!
All of 'em!
It's the New American Century!
(*Sung.*) This is the moment
of the great push
to realize our Manifest Destiny.

MOHAMMED
And am I now a part of
this destiny?

MR DIRECTOR
You're gonna help us
achieve it, buddy.

MRS PRESIDENT
How will he do that?

MR DIRECTOR
I'm going to send him to
Guantanamo Bay as our mole.
You're going on holiday Mr Mo!

MRS PRESIDENT
You're off to Cuba Mr Mo!

MOHAMMED
Boat rides, surfing
That is great!

MRS PRESIDENT / MR DIRECTOR
He can't wait to get to Guantanamo Bay!
He loves Camp X-Ray!

PRESIDENT and DIRECTOR leave, laughing.

Scene 8

Postlogue

MOHAMMED is left alone in the Oval office with his guards. Lights focus down onto him.

MOHAMMED
> When I betrayed Leila
> they told me where they'd sent her.
> She is there in that place.
> O how I want to face
> her and ask that she forgives me
> – and gives me redemption.

End of Act Two.

ACT THREE: THE HEIGHTS

Scene 1

Guantanamo Bay. Camp X-ray. LEILA and her JAILER.

LEILA is tied to a chair. She is dishevelled and brutalized and has bloody feet. JAILER has a small manuscript in his hand. He stands over her threateningly.

JAILER
>What is this?
>It's not poetry!

LEILA
>It's the Word!

JAILER
>The word of an infidel!

LEILA
>It is the Word!
>It is the Word!
>It is the Word!

JAILER
>The word of my enemy!

LEILA
>It is my shout for freedom! for freedom, for freedom!

JAILER
>That's propaganda!

LEILA
>But you are my jailer!

JAILER
>We are here to free you!

LEILA

Free me from what?

JAILER

From your history!
From this garbage!

He hits her viciously across the face with the manuscript. She cries out.

Your world is dead!
The future is American!
Your world enslaves us.
Our world is freedom!

He hits her repeatedly with the manuscript.

Freedom! Freedom! Freedom! Freedom!

She cries.

LEILA

Then let me die!
Please let me die.

JAILER

No! I will save you!

LEILA's head hangs low.

LEILA

There is a tree
in my mother's garden
for many a hundred year,
for many a hundred year.
Green and rich in foliage.
Now a sandstorm
has stripped
it of its bark
and stripped it of life.

JAILER returns with a bowl of water and a cloth. He places the bowl before her and gets to his knees. He wets the cloth, wrings it out and wipes her face.

JAILER
> We are not here to hurt you
> but you leave us no choice.
> It has to end, it has to end
> though the means may break my heart.

JAILER gets a bowl of water and unbinds her feet. He bathes her feet in the water.

> When this is over
> You'll walk on an American street
> for we will save you.
> When this is over
> you will remember
> the caress of my hand
> as the writing of your future.

LEILA
> When this is over...I'll be dead.

LEILA's hands are tied again and she is wheeled away on a trolley by guards.

Lights down.

Lights up on another part of the camp and MOHAMMED.

Scene 2

Waiting Area, Camp X-ray, Guantanamo.

Some days later. MOHAMMED sits alone on a chair.

MOHAMMED
> Waiting in this room,
> in this room in Guantanamo
> waiting for Leila
> waiting to excuse myself
> in her eyes, her eyes
> in her eyes, her eyes...her eyes...
> come with me,
> come with me, to America,

to America...

JAILER enters with Leila's manuscript.. He stands in silence for a moment.

JAILER

Are you Mohammed?

MOHAMMED

Yes, I am Mohammed.
I have come from the President
to save Leila.

JAILER turns away from MOHAMMED.

JAILER

How I loved that woman!
She held in her heart
all humanity's truths
and gave her life,
and gave her life
as though it were destiny.

MOHAMMED

Gave her life?

Silence.

JAILER

Hanged herself by a thread
light as an angel's wing
that would shatter
beneath your breath.

JAILER turns back to MOHAMMED and holds up manuscript.

It's all in here,
the breathing of her death.

MOHAMMED

No! Death's breathing's in her life.

MOHAMMED holds out his hand for the manuscript.

Give that to me or I shall die
In her silence.

BOTH
Leila! Leila, Leila

Lights down.

Scene 3

The Sons Of Abraham

The Studio of composer DANIEL XAVIER. He is blind.

Dawn. DANIEL is sitting alone. Doors open onto a garden. Shards of sunlight begin to filter through into the room. He gets up.

DANIEL
(*With awe.*) Today the light
comes dripping
like a honey'd thread,
first one...

He reaches out. He turns his head.

...then this other one.
(*Angrily.*) What's this?

The world not mended!
Peace still a stranger!

The intensity of light steadily increases...

Why should I have this
blessing? – and there's
another thread! –
The sun rises...
This overwhelming
web of light.

...and floods into the room. His sight returns with the rising sun.

Is Leila back? No!
Then why this
luxury of sight?
I am ashamed to see
to become whole in a fractured world.
to compose for a species
that's lost its ear
for music.
And they keep coming these threads
gathering to full sight.
And yet there is joy in my tears.

*MOHAMMED appears silhouetted against the light. He holds
Leila's manuscript.*

Who is this
partially explained person?

MOHAMMED
My name is Mohammed.
This is for you.

*He hands DANIEL the manuscript. DANIEL opens the
manuscript and reads:*

DANIEL
'Manifest Destiny'

MOHAMMED
She has written:
'we have this choice – death or love'
She died loving you.

DANIEL
I am a Jew.

MOHAMMED
I know.

DANIEL
Where will you go?

MOHAMMED
Home.

DANIEL
They will kill you.

MOHAMMED
If I'm not already dead, they can't.

MOHAMMED and DANIEL embrace.

End.

POEMS

Wesker in Machynlleth

for David and Charmian

In Machynlleth I met the writer Wesker,
Jewishly sage, discursive,
playing his desires to us like a cat intuitive of conflict.
A septuagenarian

he wondered understandably
whether writers fade with age:
lose their gifts – (as though virtue
becomes less rigorous with use?)

I said; we are all, as writers,
constrained only by our vanity
which may ambush anger and hazard.
Perhaps we come to belong

no longer becoming
– throwers of feathers
forgetting that poetry is the bomb
of the outcast; comfortable

with the specious conclusions, forgetting
that the only argument we should want
is the one that doesn't confine us
by being won.
                         So it was lunch
with Wesker bunched
with other flowers of Art's Diaspora
like the 16 year old Swedish girl

whose hunger for truth made us childish
so emphatic about what we are
with her brave stanzas – not unlike
the girls on the returning bus

announcing their arrival

with lesbo-erotic bravado
kissing brutally before phlegming up revolutionary
gobbets of thistling spit like exploding couplets.

Wesker is like a rabbi:
you can trust him to be there
for achievement though its success
echoes ever fainter with age and

new success is capricious. Perhaps
this is it, in which case Wales
– metaphor for the triumph of the schemed
over the intuited – may have been good for him

as it is for those of us here: ever cautioned
by nothing more profound than the elements
against expectation of success;
wise to surprise neglect

with presumption of it.

Impromptu

for Natalie

My daughter cried because on Christmas Eve – she's 17 –
she said she'd cook the dinner; for her first time, of course.
I say, of course of course because well...fuck that
(that's me) it was, I realise now, a more momentous
thing than simply cooking turkey, it was – though I thought
                                                    then
a way of humbling me – I think, a way of getting me
to notice her at that time, late at night, Christmas Eve,
watching Family Fortunes on Sky. She says: we'll have...
are we having sprouts? I said: No, cabbage, you said
you didn't want sprouts. She said: I thought *you* wanted
sprouts. I said: No, I'm over that. Then she said: So:
potatoes, mashed potatoes, roast potatoes, parsnips, roast
parsnips, cabbage, carrots and peas. And I said:
there's no peas, we had them today for dinner and she
said: will you go down to the shop and buy some?
I said: no, it's Christmas!
Later, she came in crying and I nearly laughed. I
couldn't believe she'd cry over peas. And she said:
Are we going to have this dinner tomorrow or what?
The first she would have cooked ever. A big day.

Ridgecruising

for Feargus

We walked where plants eat flesh:
within the mat of sphagnum moss
sundews and butterworts
trap flies to feed the vegetable beast.

Feargus placed a lamb's skull
on a proud Northern dock
in death's domain, he the lamb
defining our middle age. We

process uncertain terrain
towards memorial peaks.
This, too, is the way to relationships:
the women who have touched us

caught in marriage or partnership's
tendrils, victims of foliate gorging; memories
footprints shaped in the dust of ragged ridges.
Standing on Pen-y-Fan

with the thundering wind evacuating
the moment of reflection
might itself be a ceremony of marriage
with past lovers

for there is no certainty on ridges.
We are all struggling along escarpments
towards the final georama;
to be embraced by enlightenment

before we fall from life
freefalling, flying the gauntlet of those clapping
broken-backed loves;
                                unless, regretfully,

we spend our last moments
cracked like Mallory, up with the gods
reflecting incongruously on the shoulder
which can't rightly be called ham.

Fellfalling

for The Gutmanns

Later in the day, above Rhuthin,
I thought of your girls and
the splendid calm of their
unprepossessing presence

this morning and yesterday's evening
and the indomitable boy who shared with us
the embrace of that impetuous blizzard
that so startled the twilight

and, for a moment, brought us face to face
with Scott's incomparable
sinking feeling.
What is it about us

falling down mountains in middle-age –
hooligans to maturity –
that can capture their respect?
It is that we share the gypsy song,

the *canto hondo*
by which we are humbled and ennobled
the same; we are all children of experience
either innocent or learning the beauty

of innocence;
we are all subject to the same geometry
the same mournful soliloquies
of subverted passion;

conjuring up in some late day, wings with
ruminative or leaping descent.
we are all arrogant but only to find beauty
though pleasured by the comforts of ignorance.

And in mid-morning, the girls feed us
chocolate cake and tea;
in the door, the gypsy stands
with flannels and pegs and the saddest eyes

that ever looked into this
or any kitchen,
and as Kinder Scout falls into the valley
the gypsy sings a song of love...of love...of love...

Love

Somewhere in a time fallen
the horses gallop wild
their hooves like maracas
a train's hooter howls

freedom
stupidity
on the plains
the settlers despise the ancients

of the mountains
the ancients have place
and wisdom
but will fall from their reliquary peaks

you see the sea
you see the rainforest
you see and understand
how the glorious mountains rose

yet love sneaks up
taps your heel
and you fall
on the beach

cherry blossom
from those trees of which you hoped
Spring's insemination would confirm
fullness lies tragic

and sad, decolouring
it is the time of all falling
of blood falling of coral trinkets
falling of nightingales and mockingbirds

falling into dreams
they could not possibly dream

of the decolouring of falling
when the wild grasses disappear

what will we think about
progress or sentiment
love or desert?
Or will we say

we once made of the grasses
bracelets to hold the treasures
of invention and fullness
to save ourselves from falling

Lust

In the burning tropics of her room
beneath the gaze of the salamander
unmoved by the fire
its stoic eye the ultimate judge

he painted his death upon her back –
the little moans of her pleasure
anticipating the howling of her grief
the stillness is magnificent

locked in her as he dies
only somewhere distant beyond the house
somewhere amongst the twining liana
Berlioz' mad-struck chords

wrought from the grief made of love
– that music that executes lovers – echoes
while all through his last night
the stump-tailed loris

                            which can see in the dark
watches over their gorging on lotus